Potty Training

THROUGH PARENTING

Laura Woj

ISBN: 978-1-61244-535-9
Library of Congress Control Number: 2017906082

Printed in the United States of America

Halo Publishing International
1100 NW Loop 410
Suite 700 - 176
San Antonio, Texas 78213
Toll Free 1-877-705-9647
www.halopublishing.com
E-mail: contact@halopublishing.com

Contents

Introduction

Whenever I'm out and about and people ask me what I do, I tell them I am a potty training educator. It's remarkable how most of them have a modern-day, relevant situation! Either their own toddler is potty training, or their grandchild is potty training. And then comes the same question from everyone: What's your biggest piece of advice for me?

I always give them a quick, two-minute answer using the best of my knowledge I have at hand, but that's only because I know they need real, practical advice for that moment. Hopefully, you have some time and are not in a potty training crisis. My *real* piece of advice is this: Take time to prepare. Read this book in its entirety.

There are a ton of potty training aid books and bits out there, some telling you there is one method that works for all and some telling you that potty training takes twenty-four hours, but this book is different. It's full of practical parenting wisdom that can change how you teach your child, not just train them. It teaches you how to think things through with your child's end goal in mind, which is making them a great human governed by the morals and values of their parents. I'm happy to go on this journey with you, and I'm really excited to help you glean new insights about your amazing child! God has made each of us so unique and wonderful, and I hope to help you look into the heart of your child and find the best potty training method for your little one, yourself, and your family.

When You Think You're Getting Close

It is inevitable you will have to go through this. You certainly don't have to do this alone or unarmed! You've got a great book here that gives you more than just how to potty train, and you have support. Let me first encourage you to join our community of parents going through the same thing. You're not alone! There are hundreds of parents on our Facebook group that are actively sharing their experiences, their fears, and their triumphs. I'm there, as well. I will help you as issues arise and answer your questions. You can find me on Facebook under my public profile Laura Woj. The group we have is closed, but from here you can be let in. It is a safe, nurturing, and sweet place to be, so I hope you'll join us even if you aren't potty training yet - because you will be.

If you've already gone out and bought a toilet and undies and have had that mini potty sitting around in your living room, go put it away. Just for now. Just until you've read this book, at least. Even if your toddler has used it a few times, don't hold on to the hope that it will happen magically. Just put it away for now. If your toddler sees you do this, great! Tell him or her that you two are not ready to use this potty. It won't hurt to build a little anticipation!

Many people I come across tell me that they think their toddler is ready, but someone in their life says otherwise. This is typically another family member, like Dad or Grandma. The other side of the coin is usually Mom telling her daughter it is time to potty train, but the daughter isn't convinced (or more appropriately, she doesn't feel adequate to get the job done).

The other common misconception parents have about not being ready to potty train is the age of their toddler. For so long, they have heard that you need to be two years old, and they look at their eighteen- or twenty-month-old and just think maybe it's not time. Regardless of where you are on this scale, you are getting closer to potty training.

If you think it's time, it probably is. If you have had the sneaking suspicion that your child is capable of potty training, they probably are. And if your mom or dad is telling you their grandchild is ready, then they are seeing something you aren't seeing.

Need some more convincing? Let's assess the young potential trainers

Let's do a little exercise. I want you to consider the capabilities of your child as we go through some of the following questions and exercises:

Can your child help carry clothes from the dryer to the couch? I am not asking if she can help fold them, but can she see what you are doing, or better yet, follow a verbal cue to take some clothes, follow you, and set them on the couch?

Let's do some of these tests and see just how thick your child's understanding really is:

Sit in a room at least ten feet away from the trash can. Take a piece of paper and tell your child to come over, take the paper, throw it out, and then come back. You can point to the trash can, if needed.

Ask your child to point to objects that you have around you as you name them. These should be things that are normally in the house, like a pet, couch pillows, the floor, and the refrigerator.

Put crayons on the table and ask for the red crayon. See how many colors they know.

Start at one point in the house and have your child run from you to another room and back. Go from the living room to the bedroom and back, then from the living room to the kitchen and back.

These are simple tests that your child may or may not have failed, but feel free to use these tests as a teaching experience, as well. If you show them the different rooms in the house and then come back and have them perform this test, do you see how their understanding has already grown?

Just like that, in a matter of minutes, days, or hours, your child has begun to understand an abstract concept of a place having a title or learning colors. As I mentioned, if they aren't capable of doing these things, were they capable of learning them? Take note of how fast your child learns. This will help you know how quickly they understand what you're teaching them when it's time to potty train.

Why is potty training so scary, anyway?

Our adorable little baby is now a toddler, checking out everything. Some of you may be at the point where your child is testing everything, including your limits. Some of you may even be beyond that, where your child is digging in his heels and demanding or resisting. And so you find yourself in a place where potty training is essential and mandatory, whether it is now or in a matter of months.

The scariest part of potty training is nothing more than the unknown; it is what doesn't exist yet. How will you start? How will your child react? You may have heard some horror stories. Will you have one of your own? The best thing you can do to help yourself is to prepare, plan, and take the time to understand all the intricacies of what is happening in your child's physical and mental development. Learn the best planning practices for potty training and then decide on the method that's right for you.

But, a secondary fear in potty training is definitely, "What if my child just won't do what I say?" Great question and one you should tackle before you start! In my seminars, I often teach parents to test their child's compliance levels and work on those battles off the potty training playing field. I even write about how to fight with them! Testing compliance before potty training is the best help you can give yourself. A kid who listens and follows directions will be easier to guide through this process. To help you further in this process, at the end of each chapter I've included real questions that parents have written in on my Facebook page, along with the answers. Maybe you will relate?

Real Q&As for Laura Woj

From Jessica -

My 18 month old has gotten SO bad about fighting diaper changes. He's gone through phases like this before but he's getting bigger and harder to contain. He screams and cries with real tears. He even tried to jump off his changing pad tonight. Is this a sign that he's ready to potty train or just a phase?

12

Jessica, if you want to see if he is receptive to potty training, just grab a small potty from the store and explain it to him. See if he uses it. If so, get ready to potty train for real though! Dabbling for a long time actually reinforces the mindset that using the toilet is just one more option, and we really don't have to use it if we don't want to. Only give him the option for a day or two, then pick it back up and read on, to potty train properly. He may really crave the independence. if If so, put the mini- potty in the bathroom, explain it all to him, then leave and let him do his thing. You will be showing him that you trust him and are giving him full control over this. Eventually, you will have to step in and lead when he looses interest, so get ready!

From Julie -

My son is two and a half. Today after his nap he pooped and took his diaper off and tried to clean it up himself. He hates sitting on the toilet and will not go on the potty at all. If we put him up there it is a huge fight. I do not have any small toilets and don't want them. What should I do to start off his big boy toilet adventure?

Hi Julie, I would recommend a small toilet. The big ones can be seen as cold and scary to little people. I get that you don't want one, but this kid is in the middle of potty training himself - a place where many parents wish they were! Just grab a cheap one, or better yet - let him pick one out! If he's going to potty train himself, let him do it! Just be prepared to not allow him to slip once he's had his fill of new activities.

The Age of Potty Training

So many parents just don't feel confident in their ability to judge their child's readiness to potty train, so it's reasonable to ask for an age. If you want an Americanized short answer, the age is two and a half. If you want to think through this and see what works for your family, the age can vary dramatically! Two and a half is the best answer a pediatrician can give because it hits every cue, almost without fail. The child is capable mentally and his body is ready physically. The problem here arises if he has not been familiarized with the toilet yet. Children this age have far more reasoning capabilities that they apply to their circumstances. When you introduce potty training at this age, you come up against their rationalizing, as well as their independent streak. They can develop abstract fears that you would not be aware of. They are more sensitive to things around them, like the cat box in the bathroom or the coolness of their bum hanging out when put on a toilet. They reason differently than us because their knowledge and experiences are limited.

One of the more interesting theories behind a child's fear in potty training is that their poop feels like a part of them. They have always had it held close and it makes sense to think that what comes from you is of you. The child resists losing their poop to the cold unknown and prefers to keep it closer with a less extreme and more gradual removal - the diaper change. Reasoning like this just doesn't happen when you potty train younger. So just for a moment, forget your child's age. Let's look at some of the cues that let you know potty training is approachable.

Physical Signs of Potty Training Readiness

- Coordination has increased to easily walking or even running.
- Pulls at the diaper.
- Stays dry in a diaper through nap or for two hours during the day.
- Pees a fair amount at one time.
- Wakes up dry in the morning.
- Has regular and well-formed bowel movements. Do not attempt to potty train when bowel movement softness is not consistent.
- Hides when pooping (because he knows he has to!).

These physical signs show that the child's bladder and sphincter muscles have developed enough to hold waste in until released, and that the child is capable of getting to the potty and getting it done. Not all of these signs need to be present to successfully potty train. If you have a few of these checked off, then all you need to do is set a date!

Beyond the physical readiness, you have behavior signs that your child can potty train.

Behavioral Signs of Potty Training Readiness

- Has an interest in pleasing parents.
- Takes pride in an accomplishment.
- Watches others and is curious about the toilet.

These behavioral signs are so helpful in the potty training process. Many parents see the behavioral signs of readiness before they see all the physical signs. Capitalizing on behavioral compliance can really boost the potty training process.

I'll tell you a secret. These signs of readiness are all Americanized and developed to involve the toddler in the process. In other countries, families often initiate a parent-led potty training approach. The Gypsies that vagabond through the countryside of Europe start potty training at twelve months old. They typically live in a single wide trailer. The mother stays home all day, tending to the children and cleaning. When the child is twelve months old, the mom switches from diapers or elimination communication and completes the potty training process. She watches like a hawk and focuses solely on this task. At every inkling that her baby might pee, she rushes him to a small pot to sit on. Wash, rinse, repeat. That's it. She doesn't stop until the process is solidified in the baby's head and her toddler begins to head to the pot himself. The size of her home is on her side at just ten feet wide, but the floor space is even less. The back of the trailer houses the bed, cutting the length short as well. She is operating in a space the size of a small living room, which helps her see everything that is happening with her baby.

My point here is not to say we need to be potty training at this age, but to prove that age may be irrelevant, depending on which approach you use and what suits your family best.

Parent-led vs. Child-led

A parent-led approach is one described above. A parent initiates and follows through with the potty training process.

This is best done silently, without much involvement of the child, other than moving them where they need to be to eliminate. It is truly "training." You are shaping a new behavior at every opportunity. You don't need to ask if the baby needs to go pee. You just watch for it. When it happens, you move them to the toilet and hope you made it. Eventually, you will be successful and through repetition, the child will catch on and begin flowing with your method. You are teaching and training the physical aspect, while developing and shaping the cognitive.

Parent-led potty training is a strong, active decision that is made by the parents. If both parents are in the home, you should agree on this before starting. You will want the support of each family member to help keep watch for the signs your child is eliminating. Parent-led potty training can happen once your baby can walk. Before then, any attempt at potty training is called elimination communication. The best age to a parent-led approach is between twelve months and twenty months. After that, it is best to use a child-led approach.

A child-led approach relies heavily on the signs of readiness and the involvement of your toddler. You two become a team and work together at this! Everyone needs to be on the same page and pre-potty prep work should be initiated to help ease the transition. Having a larger transition period also helps your child prepare emotionally and mentally for what's ahead. Verbal communication is your best asset with child-led potty training.

There are three types of readiness that child specialist Magda Gerber noted for successful toilet learning:

1. Physical: Children have bladder and bowel capacity and muscle control.

2. <u>Cognitive</u>: Children are aware of the urge to poop or pee and know what they are supposed to do.
3. <u>Emotional</u>: Children more primed to let go of situations they are used to and "let go" of their waste. This can be more difficult for kids who think that their poop is a part of them.

It is the emotional aspect that many parents often overlook which can lead to potty training disasters. This is also why a parent-led approach should happen before twenty months old. At that young age, you are not battling the development of emotional reasoning, but working only with the physical and cognitive aspects.

"Verbal communication is your best asset with child-led potty training."

I did not mention verbal skills as one of my signs of readiness because it throws people off. All the signs of readiness available on the Internet today start out with verbal communication being the first item, but in fact, I believe that communication is enough. We can communicate with our children long before they are verbal. Just try some of our earlier methods of testing compliance and their level of understanding. If you are banking on a verbal cue, then you are saying you want your child to tell you when they need to use the bathroom so you can offer assistance. Honestly, they may not even need help. Let your child know it is okay to surprise you with pee in the potty. Tell them they can go anytime, just like you do!

Since most parents find themselves in this twenty- to thirty-six-month age range and will be using a child-led approach, let's look deeper into emotional readiness. This is often the last piece to develop and is the most fragile. A child with emotional reasoning who is pushed to potty train can quickly become untrusting of the process. A perceptive, bright child may sense a parent's agenda to potty train and resist when even nudged toward the toilet. We can find ourselves in a battle of wills that we are not ready for. So how can we get our children prepped for potty training? Take it slowly and prepare for it. Take transitions more seriously and think them through.

"A child with emotional reasoning who is pushed to potty train can quickly become untrusting of the process."

Transitions and Pre-potty Prep

A transition is a change from one place to another or one thing to another. Transitions happen all the time, but they can be particularly hard on young children. Watching how your child adjusts to transitions can help you predict how they will behave in future scenarios and can help you set your child up for success.

There are so many things that all come together with potty training, that it can easily overwhelm a toddler. The urge, running for the toilet, getting your pants down, sit and aim (don't miss or pee out of the toilet!), wiping, and finally, hand washing. Yeah, that's a lot! I can see now why Johnny decided to quit participating in a day or two of all this! The best way we can get our two- and three-year-olds to be on our team is to actually make them part of The Team. We start potty training by telling him he will go without diapers tomorrow. Then, we think it's all on us to watch and redirect. But, that isn't the best way to deal with an emotionally charged, intelligent kid.

By making them part of the team, you need to plan with them, prep with them, and make them responsible for some of it. You need to have many conversations about the future. Prep them for the unknown, so they aren't scared of it when it happens. I've broken down the pre-potty prep section into two parts to make the transition as smooth as possible, verbal and physical. Plan on pre-potty prep work taking two to four weeks before you set your no-more-diapers date.

Physically Prep for Potty Training

Head-shoulders-knees-and-toes: Sing this song with the body movements often! It helps kids develop the coordination needed to get their pants down.

Hand washing: Create a routine around hand washing and make sure your child can reach the faucet. A step stool and water extender clipped to your sink's faucet can really help!

Let them dress themselves: Make sure you slow life down a bit and budget extra time for your child to learn how their clothing works. Let them dress themselves every morning and undress every night. When accidents occur later on, this will be a handy reminder for them to be more mindful of using the bathroom. Oftentimes, children don't want to stop playing or watching TV to go potty, so they have an accident. By making them come away from their activity for a longer period of time to change clothes and clean up, they will soon learn it would be faster to just go to the bathroom in the first place.

Verbally Prep for Potty Training

Start potty talking! The more you discuss and teach, without actually letting your child use the toilet, the more ready and excited they will be to start. Many of your conversations will be the building blocks of your team plan. Remember, you're not doing this without them! Help them to reason through many of these questions, but give them plenty of time to think and talk before you provide answers. I've listed some questions you can use as a guide and provided some basic notes of what response you will be trying to hit on. What does it feel like when you have to go pee?

Talk about how it might tingle. Or maybe you get a tickle below your tummy. At this stage in your child's development, he has never had to hold in urine, so talking about this will seem foreign at first. Tell him to let you know as soon as his diaper gets wet. Then, as you change it, ask if he noticed how it felt when he peed or right beforehand.

What does it feel like when you have to go poop?

Talk about the pressure you feel in your bottom end. Explain what pressure is. How it feels like something is pushing inside your backside to come out. There could also be a grumble in your lower tummy.

What are the benefits of not being in diapers anymore?

Talk about smells. When you use the bathroom, no one has to smell your poop. You have to use the bathroom if you want to go to school. All adults and big kids do this. Going potty is also faster than getting your diaper changed, so you get to play more. You stay cleaner. You don't get rashes and nothing hurts or itches down there.

How will we change from diapers to the toilet?

Talk about how he needs to learn how to use the bathroom properly and that you will help him. You will teach him how to pull his pants down, how to wipe, and how to wash his hands. This is where you two will talk about making a plan to wake up one day and try to use the potty all day. There won't be diapers and you may have accidents, but you will help him and everything will be fine.

What will it feel like if you have an accident?

Make sure you prepare your child for the sensations of an accident! Peeing is the most common first accident and can really freak a kid out! Trickle warm water down their arm and explain how if they pee in their pants, warm water will spill down their leg. It could even get his feet wet! Show him how wetness makes his clothes darker.

Talk about how poop accidents will be messy, but you will help him clean up. Tell him to let you know as soon as he feels like he needs to poop. At this point, we are still in diapers and he is free to poop in the diaper. Your goal is to change all wet or dirty diapers as soon as they get used and have a dialogue about the future. Poop will go in the potty. The diaper stopped the poop from getting on his legs and clothes, but without a diaper he wants to make sure he sits on the potty or it will be messy.

How will we handle accidents?

When there is an accident, no one gets mad. Every time you mess up, there is an opportunity to learn and try again. Start pointing out your mistakes and what you learn from them. I once swept the floor and left the pile of dust and dirt in a corner, instead of picking it up (I'm sure no one else has ever done this). My bunny hopped right through it and made a mess. I had to clean it up again because I didn't finish my job the first time. Did you forget to water a plant and now it is shriveling up? Did you leave too late for something and now you are late? Did a meal get burned? Did someone trip because they weren't paying attention? Any dialogue you have about mistakes should include what you did wrong, what you learned or observed from it, and what you could do instead. This will help set the groundwork for potty training accidents. By pointing out your flaws and even your toddler's mistakes over a period of time, you will be undoing the shame a child feels about accidents when it's potty time. Kids need help developing the emotions necessary to handle their own mistakes. These discussions should be random and daily. Mistakes happen all the time, but we don't quit just because we messed up! Having a phrase you repeat will help mentally prepare him and can transfer to potty training accidents.

Something like, "I'm not perfect, but I'm trying," might work. Or maybe, "I messed that up, but I'll get it right eventually." Repeat this when you mess up, so your child can see that mistakes aren't a big deal and life goes on. You will be thrilled when he repeats it after a potty training accident! (It helps when learning to ride a bike too.)

How will we use the potty when we leave the house?

This is actually a plan you two will develop. You can plan to potty before leaving. You can ask your toddler if he is brave enough to use the big potties when out. You can even head into the restrooms of a department store, just to see what the toilets are like. Or sneak away from the table in a restaurant to investigate what the bathroom is like in a place like that. Don't forget to hear what they sound like when they flush!

Checking out the different toilets and bathrooms while your toddler is still in diapers will, again, build anticipation of the time he will get to try and use them. Your toddler can make the decision though. If he wants to try the bigger toilets, great! Put a sticky note over the auto flush sensor, so it doesn't go off on him. If he decides that it is too scary, talk about traveling with a smaller potty and using it in the car.

Is having an accident bad?

Accidents or mistakes just give us a chance to grow. We learn from everything that goes wrong! Accidents are not bad. Everybody makes mistakes all the time. No one is perfect. I can't stress this enough. Prepare your child for mistakes. He is making mistakes constantly already and it always turns out okay.

When will we start to use the toilet?

This is where the two of you set a date. You can teach her the abstract concept of how each square on the calendar represents a day. Make notes on your calendar of the big toddler things that happened on certain days. Monday, you went to the park. Tuesday, you visited grandma. Wednesday, you got pizza. Thursday, you got to paint. By going over the special parts of each day while pointing to the calendar blocks, you are teaching about time. Days start and end. Every block has a morning, then lots of fun, then we go to bed. The next block is the next day.

After some studying of the calendar, you two will be able to set a day to ditch the diapers. She will be able to see it coming. Her transition will be so much smoother when you visit the calendar daily!

Not everything is open for discussion. We want to empower our children to be part of the Potty Team, but sometimes you will call the shots. You are ultimately the Team Lead. Things like how often your child visits the potty and how long they sit there will be decided by you. You will have a better sense of these things. Explain that they will get to make some choices and you will get to make some choices.

"By pointing out your flaws and even your toddler's mistakes over a period of time, you will be undoing the shame a child feels about accidents when it's potty time. Kids need help developing the emotions necessary to handle their own mistakes."

From Serena G.

Okay. This is gonna be a tough one! My stepson is going to be 3 tomorrow, and his father and I think he's ready to start potty training! We have gauged his interest, and we both think it's time…here's the kicker: bio mom won't do it…not getting into the details. Anyway, we only have him right now from Friday night till Sunday night and Wed. night. Is it even possible for us to potty train in a weekend and then send him home? He will go pee every time I sit him on it. He will not tell me if he has to go pee. He has pooped on it but won't tell us he has to.

Dear Serena,

Age is on your side! Since he is almost three, he can certainly potty train in your time frame. AND if you have many discussions about not using the diaper anymore—EVEN IF HE IS WEARING ONE—then you can help him potty train himself when he leaves your care. Start potty training at your house with no diaper for the first day, but tell him you will be playing a game with him the next day. On day two, tell him you will put a diaper on him, but you want him to take it off and go to the potty. Incentivize this behavior heavily, even if it is just with a mini- dance party when he does it. This will teach him to stay potty training when in a diaper at his mom's house. Your potty training just has to incorporate independence into it so he can stay on his program when he's gone. But either way, you enforce the rules at your house.

Be Nice To You

Before potty training, you must be prepared to be nice to you. Think about the things that are stressors in your life and get ready to give yourself a few free passes. I like to tell parents, "Make it frozen pizza night or even frozen pizza week!" The high expectations of running a household don't NEED to be perfectly upheld in this time. Here's some ways you can just be nice to you.

Laundry - Save it all up and drop if off at a fluff and fold. It's about $1 per pound. Many people don't even THINK about this, but it could be invaluable to your peace of mind. Laundry is the number one non-financial domestic nightmare of family life. Or maybe you have a friend or relative that can agree to come help for a few weeks?

Dinner time - Make dinners easy. I'm not a microwave person myself, but if you are, then now is the time to use it! Frozen pizzas, take-and-bake lasagne, the fresh deli bar at the grocer, and take home sub sandwiches are all great options to consider when planning your menu.

Cleaning - If you are the typical cleaning person, then I have something to share with you. You may be cleaning even more during your potty training career. You have a few options though. Enlist the help of your spouse to help! If you do this, then please make it easier on them by making a list of things you need help with. That way, they don't feel like you are telling them what to do (like you're the boss) and the work is quantified. List things like "Sweep kitchen" instead of "Sweep up" and "Wash towels and jeans" instead of "Do laundry" or "Empty dishwasher and reload" rather than "Do dishes." Vague references to work leave the job open for interpretation and your idea of "Do laundry" may entail wash, dry, fold, and put away, while theirs looks like wash, dry, and leave in dryer. This is where stress comes in and fights can happen. Just be kind and clear on your list.

Another idea is hire a service for once a week or every other week cleaning. Then, if the floors get dirty, you know it will be handled.

And one last thought. Only do what's necessary in this time. Laundry and dishes are typical essentials of life, but maybe sweeping, mopping, wiping cabinets, and scrubbing toilets can wait. (Do people really do all that on a regular basis??)

TRUE YOU time - You may find yourself completely overwhelmed with kid considerations during potty training. It takes up SO MUCH of your mental working capacity to constantly be watching the clock, checking pants for signs of wetness, and sitting and entertaining a kid for ten minutes at a shot that by nighttime - you're done. Make sure that you have something to do that YOU want to do and make sure your spouse is on board with that and will give you the space you need. It could be reading a good book, quilling, needlecraft, a video game, scrapbooking, journaling, drawing, coloring in your adult coloring book, gardening, or even visiting a museum! Think about the things you REALLY enjoy that you typically don't have time for and make them happen. I even put a headlamp on to tend to my garden at night. I can't seem to find the time for it during daylight hours, but I'll be darned if that's going to stop me! One TRUE YOU session a week can do wonders for your mental health!

My point is, be nice to you. Don't keep this a secret from your spouse though! Explain that things could look different and you are being nice to you and that they should be nice to you too. But, all for a great cause!

How Entitlement Affects Potty Training

When my first child was young, it was my desire as a parent to empower him, to make him feel like he mattered and had a voice! I wanted him to have a strong sense of self to develop his passions and hobbies. I listened to him, guided him, and parented him as best I could, but in my ignorance and innocence, I created a little monster.

Empowering can turn to entitlement very quickly. I gave him so many options and choices, in way too many circumstances. He became bossy and disobedient. That independence I tried to teach him was folly without knowledge, wisdom, and self-control. I later realized that a child does not develop self-control until much later in life and it was solely my responsibility to make choices for him or only allow him to make choices from appropriate options. This wasn't a free-for-all game of life with no limits and boundaries anymore. Long before potty training, you need to get a handle on who is really in control of the home.

Discipline is a harsh word if you aren't familiar with it. I always considered it to go hand in hand with punishment, but eventually, I came to see things a different way. Where discipline came with benefits!

Discipline is like this: Imagine a ride at an amusement park where there is a car you get to drive, but it is locked onto rails. You can control the car and never hit the rails, but you cannot run amok and mow down innocent bystanders because the rails keep you in check. That and the reduced speed keep you from hurting yourself and others if you happen to ram into the back of the tiny, timid driver in front of you.

Discipline is the rail on the track. A punishment or consequence is the outcome of not following the discipline that has been laid out. Some consequences are natural and some will have to be parent-induced when needed.

Now, I happen to be an animal lover who at any point in time has between ten and twenty-five pets, always with a few exotics in the mix. Don't worry. Many of them are chickens. This is my hobby and one of my passions. So, as a responsible pet owner, I feel that animals need to have some semblance of training to thrive in a home environment (especially when you have so many). When I began studying animal training, I came across this saying: "A well-trained dog gets a long leash." It can be disastrous for a potty training educator like myself to use dog training in conjunction with people training or potty training, mainly because some people in theaudience have a tendency to jump straight to the assumption that I just called their child a dog.

Not true, though, so hear me out! This saying has nothing to do with dogs. It has to do with an individual who knows what is right or wrong.

A dog who knows never to eat people food will not jump up on the coffee table and steal your snack when you walk away, so you will never have to go into a knee-jerk, disciplinary reaction with that animal and make it into a big thing. A dog that has good people manners won't run up to someone and jump on them. A dog that is properly socialized will never be the instigator of a dog park fight and will very rarely ever even be involved in one. See, a well-trained dog doesn't need a leash at all, because you trust him. You have taught him well and he learned, so now he can reap the benefits of sniffing farther without being leashed.

Now consider people. A teenager who knows the dangers of fast driving and underage drinking will be more trustworthy when they ask if they can stay out thirty minutes later. A child who is taught never to lie—no matter what—will be the one everyone listens to when there is a fight on the playground. A woman I knew had her son call her from a payphone and ask to be picked up from a party because some of the kids pulled out marijuana. He was uncomfortable and wanted to go home. This is every parent's dream and it is completely attainable with discipline and empowerment.

Discipline empowers people. Established discipline morphs naturally into self-control. This is the track we want to be on when we are looking at parenting our toddlers. A toddler who can put his clothes in a drawer and regularly helps by sweeping (even if it's not a great job) and clearing the table will be more confident in his abilities to do what you ask when you want him to use the potty. You will also be more confident in believing that he understands what you are asking of him because you've already gone through some abstract things and he understood them.

Ultimately, this is where you want to be. You want to be confident that you can do this, that you can lead your child to an independent enough state that they can get to the bathroom on their own and get the job done.

It is not too early to start. In fact, if you feel like you aren't sure if you've done an excellent job in providing clear discipline and creating an empowering environment, take a few weeks to establish this connection with your toddler before you begin potty training and you will have a much easier time of it.

Now, in contrast, waiting to develop guidelines for the discipline in your house while still providing for your children's needs and wants can quickly turn into entitlement and that will always lead back to bargaining. They will do what you ask if you do for them. We inadvertently teach this at a young age by soothing a kid with an alternative when he cries about not getting his way. Here are some examples of how we can be teaching entitlement, rather than empowerment.

Johnny doesn't want to leave the park, so he cries. Mom immediately offers him ice cream and tells him he can have it as soon as they get home!

Bella wants a big stuffed animal from the store, but it is expensive. Dad buys her a little one instead, even though there is no occasion for getting a toy and this wasn't part of the plan.

Jules doesn't want to go to the store with his parents, so they tell him if he is good throughout the trip he can get a chocolate bar. Even worse, he gets his chocolate bar even if he did cause some problems.

Molly doesn't want to clean up her toys, so Mom immediately offers to help.

In all these scenarios, there was an unwilling child who received a benefit for that attitude. The parents never just said, "Too bad!" You can actually say "too bad" in a nicer way. How about, "Sorry honey, this is just the way it is."

I once asked The Boy (who is now a teenager) to bring in the groceries from the car, so he told me to hold the door open for him. I asked him to bring in groceries because I didn't want to do itand I did the chore of shopping and paying! I'm not about to stand there while he makes a trip back and forth and wastes my time. He wanted me to give a little if he was going to give a little.

That's not the way it works. Parents get to tell kids what to do. It's one of our benefits of having them. We pay for everything and carry a great deal of responsibility for them. They should be helping out and they should know how not to throw a fit if they have to go grocery shopping, even if they don't have an iPad in their hands.

Discipline is getting out of bed when the alarm goes off. It's putting things away after you're done using them. It's forcing yourself to get out of bed and turn the hall light off, so it's not on all night. It's folding the clothes in the dryer, instead of letting them sit there. In a nutshell, discipline is doing what you don't want to do. That is as basic a term I can give. You don't feel like it, but you know you should, so you do. Can you begin to see how a child who has experience with discipline can take to potty training with fewer problems?

Here are a few symptoms of entitlement that you can use to self-evaluate whether you are raising an entitled toddler:

Your child …
1. Often tells you "no."
2. Seems bossy.
3. Is often unsatisfied.
4. Expects bribes for good behavior.

5. Needs a treat to get through a store.
6. Always seems to want more.

Here are some good examples to help you evaluate if your disciplinary guidelines are working well:

Your child …
1. Readily helps when asked.
2. Can handle disappointment well.
3. Is generally obedient.
4. Stays confident when left at daycare, with a babysitter, etc.
5. Can shop without asking for things.
6. Can be patient (sit or wait for five minutes) without an electronic device to sooth them.

All this being said, an entitled child will feel so completely in control of their own body and life that potty training will not happen on your terms. Almost 100 percent of the time when an older three-year-old or a four-year-old is not potty trained, entitlement is the cause. They have been given too much power in the family. Undoing entitlement and bringing healthy discipline into a child's life should be done off the potty training field before potty training is introduced.

"Discipline is doing what you don't want to do. You don't feel like it, but you know you should, so you do. Can you begin to see how a child who has experience with discipline can take to potty training with fewer problems?"

Realistic Toddler Jobs

Put toys away - Be sure to clarify that toys go in certain places. Teach them what goes on a shelf, what goes in a bin, or what sits on the floor. Making a small picture chart and hanging it on the door is a great way of reminding them. You could draw a bed with stuffed animals on it, a shelf with trucks, and so on.

Sweeping the floor - You could also take this a step further and have them vacuum up the pile they swept. Dustpans are hard to use for little ones.

Floor monitor - This chore involves the ownership of a specific floor, like the living room. Explain that the floor should be cleared up every night (before dinner or before bed would be a great time). At that cued time, they are to clear the floor, put everything in its place, and throw away trash. The floor could be their bedroom, but could also be a common space that you also view often so you can help them in their training period. Just make sure there is really stuff that collects on that floor so it is a proper job, even if you stage it and plant things there to reinforce the behavior.

Washing windows - Kids find this job so fun! Put it on your calendar (or phone reminder) for once a week and make sure you hit the dirtiest, most commonly used windows and sliders first.

Zoo keeper - This person feeds the pets. In my house, it isn't just a toddler's job anymore though! My eleven-year-old is responsible for feeding the goats every morning and night, gathering the eggs, checking the chickens' grain, and feeding the dog. When he was a toddler, it was just feeding and watering the dog. Zoo keeper can be broken up and divided by animals too. My six-year-old takes care of the bunny. The children have always cared for the animals since they were in their toddlerhood and this has helped them learn responsibility, but also to empathize with creatures. I always follow up of course, to prevent any disaster.

Gardener - This ambitious little tyke learns the difference between weeds and which plants we want. You then teach him to play "Godzilla" and go through ripping the weeds out of the garden and grass and putting them into a paper bag for disposal.

Condiment captain - This job happens after dinner. The condiment captain is responsible for putting away any condiments (ketchup, salad dressing, salt, pepper, butter) in the proper place. I have even gone so far as to label shelves in my refrigerator with what goes where. As a family, we never have dessert until the table is cleaned. Each of my children are responsible for a chore. One is condiment captain, one is the table wiper (after it is cleared), and one clears dishes. Each person rinses and loads their own dishes, so only pots remain. If I had a fourth child, I would make one the leftover king! Someone who is in charge of putting away leftovers! Since I do most of the cooking, it's great to sit back and watch my minions do the rest, then serve us all dessert!

Napkin captain - Responsible for putting a napkin at each person's chair. Evolve this job to include utensils, to show your toddler he can do even more! He can even help decide what utensils are needed, based on the meal the family will eat. By letting him see or know what is cooking and talk about the utensils needed, it will also ease the transition of trying a new food and help make a toddler less of a picky eater.

Table wiper - This is a simple job, but the child still needs to be trained properly, so they don't just wash food onto the floor. It is also one that is easy to monitor and has natural accountability built in, since dinner is something that happens every day. A plus for those of us that have a hard time with follow-up items, like me!

How to Talk and What to Say
(Helpful conversations to have)

You will find these topics in a few different areas of the book, particularly, The Elimination Game. Regardless of potty training, these are great topics to cover with your kids that will help them see the world from a more educated perspective. I've given a small write-up of how a conversation might go with your child, but I've also included the goal of the conversation. You can use your own words. Just try and hit that goal. You can also just read what I wrote, then go over it. See if your toddler has any questions. These conversations should be had both casually as reminders and in an eyeball to eyeball fashin. You want to make sure the information is getting through to them. These conversations will be the building blocks of future potty training.

When having a conversation with a verbal kid, make sure it becomes just that - a conversation. Ask questions to test their understanding. For example, when discussing how everyone uses the toilet, follow up with, "Who uses the toilet?" Let them respond. Ask more questions to engage their critical thinking. Do puppies use the toilet? Do ants use the toilet? Does the grocery store worker use the toilet? You want to show them that everyone eliminates in a fashion that is appropriate to that creature. All ants, everywhere, eliminate the same way. So do people.

When having a conversation with a non-verbal child, engage them with prompted responses. Ask them to point to things like pictures or body parts in response. You want to check their understanding, while still engaging their critical thinking. Things like "Can you show me the toilet?", "Do you know where the toilet paper is?", and "Who around here uses the toilet?" are all good questions to prompt a non-verbal response.

Diapers - No going back

Once we start The Elimination Game, we will stop using diapers in the daytime. We will still pee and poop in the daytime though. We will do the same thing as we did in the diaper, but we will do it in the potty instead. There will be plenty of accidents, but that doesn't mean we will go back into diapers. We will just clean them up and try again.

The goal:
- To get your toddler understanding there will be no more diapers, no matter what.
- To reduce the chance of regression.
- To sets expectations that no more diapers will now be the "normal way".

Accidents - There will be plenty of accidents

An accident is when we pee or poop and it didn't get in the toilet. It will happen, but when it happens we will learn from this. "When you have an accident, you have to tell me right

away. We will clean it up after we try and sit on the toilet."
Accidents help us learn.

What an accident feels like

If you pee and don't have a diaper on, you will get wet. It will make your clothes wet and the wetness will spread. It might get your legs, feet, or shoes wet, as well. If the pee gets on your skin, it will be warm at first, but then it will make you cold. There might be a puddle on the floor. For boys, the water will spray out from the body. You will be able to see it. If any of this happens, you have to know that you are peeing. We need to get to the toilet before this happens.

If you poop without a diaper on, you will feel something warm and heavy in the back of your underwear or pants. If you aren't wearing anything, this warm poop will plop on the floor. It needs to be cleaned up correctly, so don't touch it. Just tell me (show me) what happened and we will go handle it together. We will use toilet paper and try to pick it up, then go flush it down the toilet. You can do the flushing! The poop could hit your leg on the way down to the floor. We will have to wash you up. If this happens, you need to try to get to the potty before it comes out next time. The potty will catch it for us. This is what we always want to happen. We want the potty to catch things now, instead of the diaper.

Do This Demonstration

Explain that urine is watery. This is what makes the inside of their diapers wet, but they may not be able to feel the wetness. Take some water and have them pour it into a diaper. Explain this is what the inside of a wet diaper looks like. When there is no diaper, this wetness will go on the floor, on their legs, on things, and on clothing if it doesn't go into the potty.

Now, take a small amount of warm water and have them pour it on a pair of pants that they are not wearing. You can even discuss where their anatomy lines up with the pants and have them pour it there. Watch how the wetness spreads in the cloth. Wait a bit and feel how the temperature changes.

Now, take more water, about how much your child can pee, and do the same thing. Show how more water spreads farther.

You can now ask if your child wants to feel what it will be like by wearing a dry pair of pants and having the water be poured there. Explain this is what an accident is. An accident is when they eliminate without getting it in the toilet.

The goal:
- To prep children for accidents, so they are not shocked (which can lead to resistance) when one happens.
- To normalize accidents and eliminate any shame behind them. Accidents are bound to happen and will be used for learning.

Urge sensation

Inside your tummy is a balloon called the bladder. It can feel things, just like your fingers feel things. When your bladder has enough drinks in it (milk, water, juice, or whatever your child commonly drinks), it starts to tingle. When your body feels this tingle, it will start to pee. At some point in the day, you will feel this tingle, but so far you probably have been ignoring it.

The tingle goes away as soon as you pee. It doesn't matter when you pee if you have a diaper on, because the diaper is always there to catch it. When you don't have a diaper on, you will need to pay attention to that tingly feeling. I can't feel your tingle. Only you can. Try and see if you can feel it today and then pay attention to how it goes away as you pee.

Before you poop, there will be a pushing feeling inside your bottom end. It is your body telling you that the poop needs to go out. Your body is all done with it and needs to get rid of it. When you feel this pressure (or pushing), you always go poop afterwards. The diaper catches it, but when you aren't wearing a diaper, you will need to get to the toilet before you let the poop out. I'm excited to see if you can feel this pressure before you poop!

The goal:
- To start to bring awareness to the sensations necessary for a person to get to the bathroom in time.
- To reduce the chances of withholding poop, an occurrence where a child chooses not to poop because of anxiety.
- To reduce the chances of your child hiding to poop.
- To eliminate any anxiety over these sensations by calling attention to them and learning about them before a child has to figure it out on their own.

Everyone uses the toilet - everyone

All over the world, everyone uses the toilet. Everything and everybody that is alive has to eat and drink. Everyone who eats and drinks will need to eliminate. (Use your own terms. I use pee and poop, but obviously you should use your terms and be consistent.) Talk about how people you know go to the bathroom and shut the door. Behind the door, they are sitting on the toilet and peeing or pooping. Point out people on TV and tell them that each person uses the toilet. Family. Teachers. Celebrities. Use people they can identify with. Kids or hosts on children's shows. Aunts and uncles. Does sister use the potty? Yes. Even the dog goes potty. Animals don't use toilets, but people do. They always do. Do some guessing games about what goes potty. Does the chair poop? Does the car poop? Does the cat poop? Does a tiny little ant poop? You have been peeing and pooping your whole life, but always in a diaper. Babies who can't walk need to use diapers because they can't get to a toilet, but as people grow up, they have to start using a toilet.

The goal:
- Normalize bodily functions.
- Teach that everything living has to eliminate.
- Engage critical thinking over animate and inanimate objects.
- Show that your child will not be exempt from this process.
- Ease the transition of not using a diaper by explaining why.

Big and little potty

We will use a little potty at first, because you are so little. It will be quicker for you to get to. We can move the small potty around with us, take it in the car, and put it in whatever room we are in. We need a small toilet because we cannot move the big toilet around, but when you pee or poop in it, we will still dump the little potty stuff into the big potty. Then, we will flush it away. When you've had enough practice at going potty, you can use the big potty too! We will have a step stool to help you climb up, but I want to use the little potty first until you get used to it. Our toilet here in the bathroom is big, but the toilets in stores are even bigger! Big toilets make a loud sound. You just have to get used to it. The toilets in stores make an even louder sound! We'll check it out so you can see what I'm talking about. It's just how they work.

The goal:
- To point to the small toilet as a travel tool and prep them for using it when you're out.
- To help the child understand another transition will be ahead.
- To create curiosity about toilets outside the home and prepare them for their use.

Food and drink turn to pee and poop

Our body needs food and water to grow. It's so cool how this happens, but our stomach mashes up everything we eat and drink and separates it all. All the liquid goes one way and all the food goes another way. The body takes out all the color from our food and drink and uses whatever it can from it. When our bodies are done, our poop is brown and our pee is yellow or clear. Poop always comes out the back and pee always comes out the front (for boys or the center for girls). Our poop is really just food that our body is done using. It's called waste. This is our body's way of throwing out the food and the toilet is like a trash can for our body's waste. Poop and pee are really just our body's garbage. Everyone's waste is the same color, because everyone's body does the same thing.

The goal:
- To make the connection between food and waste.
- To help explain why poop is brown and why it doesn't look like food.
- To reduce the chance that your child may think the poop is a part of him, which causes fear and anxiety when eliminating it. More problems can grow from this thought process.

Do this fun demonstration

In preparation for them to understand how poop works, tell your child you want to show her something. Show your child a banana and ask if she ever eats them. When she says yes, get a bowl out and tell her you want to show her what happens when she does. Tell her the bowl is her stomach. Unpeel the banana and place it in a bowl. Does she chew the banana? Give her a fork and tell her the fork is like our teeth. She can have fun mashing the banana up. Talk to her about what she is seeing. The fork (our teeth) "chews" the food, so it turns into smaller pieces. Making our food smaller helps it fit through our body because all our food has to come out at some point.

But there is only a little opening for your body to push it out, so we need to make sure our food gets chewed well. Leave the mashed up pile in the middle of the bowl.

Food has good things in it that our body needs. We can't live without food and our body tells us that it wants more food by making us hungry. Our stomach needs time to squish the banana around and get all the vitamins, minerals, fat, carbs, and protein out of it. Tell her we need to leave the banana in the bowl (our stomach) for a while and come back to see what happens. You can come back throughout the day and even leave it on the counter overnight. Try and draw out the color change that happens. See if your child can pick up on any changes in the banana.

Showing your child a food that goes from light to dark (brown) will help them relate how the brown of our poop is really just old food.

You can do this experiment every single day with other things if you want to drive the point home. Mashed up apples turn brown, too. You could put some bread in a bowl, pour some apple juice on it, wait for it to get all soggy, and then mash it up with something else. I guarantee your toddler will love this experiment and repetition is the best way to teach children.

The more poop talk we have regarding the food-to-poop relationship, the easier pooping on the toilet will be. It is important that you combat the idea that poop is a part of your child and make poop about nothing more than old food. Children often think that pooping feels like they are losing a part of themselves and will freak out without this knowledge.

What are germs?

Germs are tiny "bugs" that live on all things. They are so tiny you can't even see them! Some germs are supposed to stay in a certain place and if they go where they shouldn't, they can cause trouble. Germs are very sticky and can easily stick from one thing to another when the two touch. Your butt has germs and your poop has those same germs because it comes from your butt. These germs aren't supposed to be anywhere except there. If those butt germs get on your hands or accidentally in your mouth, it can make you feel sick. That's why we put them in the toilet. That's also why babies wear diapers. Parents don't want those butt germs getting anywhere they aren't supposed to be. The germs in your butt are fine and healthy there, but if they get into your mouth or into your vulva, they can make you sick. They start to fight with the germs that are supposed to be there and sometimes they win. You body needs the different germs to stay where they are. Germs from your pee area won't hurt you if they move to your backside, but germs from your backside will cause trouble if they get to your pee area. That is why we wipe from front toward the back. If you wipe from back toward the front you could be smearing your butt germs where they shouldn't be. This is why we wash our hands after we wipe, use the bathroom, or clean up an accident. We could have butt germs on our hands without even knowing it, but soap gets them all off.

Do this demonstration

This explanation of germs works well with more than two people, so enlist some help. You could host a play date or bring in your partner or other family members.

Recap how our body makes waste and that waste has germs on it that need to stay where they are. These germs can come from many places, not just our waste. Germs can come from our mouth and nose, as well. Germs are fine and healthy if they stay in the places they are made. They are not allowed to get to other places or we could accidentally ingest them and that could make us sick. We can't see germs because they are too small, but let's just pretend we can. Take a vial of fine glitter (or perhaps flour, but glitter would ultimately be more readily seen after playing) and tell them this will be our pretend germs. Sprinkle some into your hands and do a fake sneeze into your cupped hands. Show everyone your hands so they can see the germs! Feel free to wipe your nose if you'd like.

Now, introduce yourself to someone and shake hands. See how sticky germs are? Have kids shake hands back and forth. Play with some toys together, touch some door knobs, drink from a glass. Now, make a plate of crackers for the group, but don't eat them! After making the plate, you can inspect them to see if you can find any glitter on them. When you feel like you've spread enough glitter, stop and ask the kids to find the germs. Having a four- or five-year-old present for this activity really helps. They have a way of saying things in kid-terms and younger children really focus on the older ones. As you know, the glitter will spread and "contaminate" may things. And that's how germs spread!

The goal:
- To teach kids about germs.
- To connect body waste with germs.

Waste is the body's trash

We don't play in the trash because it has stuff in it that could be dirty or have germs. When we are done with something or when we can't use it anymore, we throw it out. We try not to touch the trash, because this is where lots of dirty things go. The poop and pee is our body's trash, so we try not to touch that too. Sometimes, we need to if we have an accident. We will have to clean it up and get it in the right place. If we do touch our body's waste, we just need to wash our hands afterwards.

The goal:
- Reinforce that our body's waste is trash and needs to be disposed of.

The toilet is for bodily waste and toilet paper only

That's it. We don't throw anything away in the toilet except for our body's waste and toilet paper. If you have any other trash, it goes in the trash can. The toilet is a special trash can that takes our body's waste to a place where it won't make anything dirty. Nothing else goes in the toilet, ever. Never put a toy in it or a piece of paper or a broken crayon. Those things will break the toilet. You can't even put your diaper in it. Diapers need to be thrown out. They are too big for the toilet.

The goal:
- To combat the inevitable. When kids start to become aware of the potty, they flush stuff down it.

Why we wear underwear

When we are using the toilet, we still have germs that need to stay in their place. Underwear keeps the germs from our backside and between our legs, where they should be. Sometimes after wiping, we may not have gotten all the germs off. That's okay though. We just use underwear to keep the germs from getting on our clothes. When we take a bath, we are washing any germs off that are hanging around from the day. We change our underwear every day. Adults and kids wear underwear. They aren't like a diaper though, but putting underwear on might feel like a diaper. Underwear won't stop an accident and you should not pee or poop in it.

The goal:
- To instill good hygiene routines.
- To normalize the thinner, non-diaper garment.
- To reduce the chance that your child will be potty trained when naked, then eliminate in undies or when they wear clothes.

Hand washing

Whenever we go potty, we need to wash our hands afterwards. While we are wiping and while we are dumping the little potty into the bathroom toilet, we could get waste germs on us, so we need to be sure to wash that off. Even if your hands look clean, you have to wash. Remember, germs are invisible, so we can't see them.

Do This Demonstration

Smear your hands with butter or Vaseline and have your toddler do the same. Try to be a bit sneaky and get some of this grease between the fingers and backs of hands. Then, have someone sprinkle your hands with cinnamon. This is the stickiness of germs and dirt. Rinse your hands first with cold water. Check if you can still see a bit of stuff left. Next, try soap and warm water. See how soap and warm water is key. Did we get between the fingers and the backs of hands? Those germs can be sneaky, so we have to be thorough when washing. Soap will be the powerhouse here. If you have trouble getting anything off, just use more soap.

The goal:
- Promote good hygiene.
- Demonstrate proper hand washing skills.

Foamy colored soap might be fun for toddlers to engage them in hand washing. They might love it so much that they want to wash all the time! If so, establish when hands need to be washed, instead of leaving it up to the toddler to decide. Times like arriving home, after using the bathroom, before eating, and after eating are all great hand washing times.

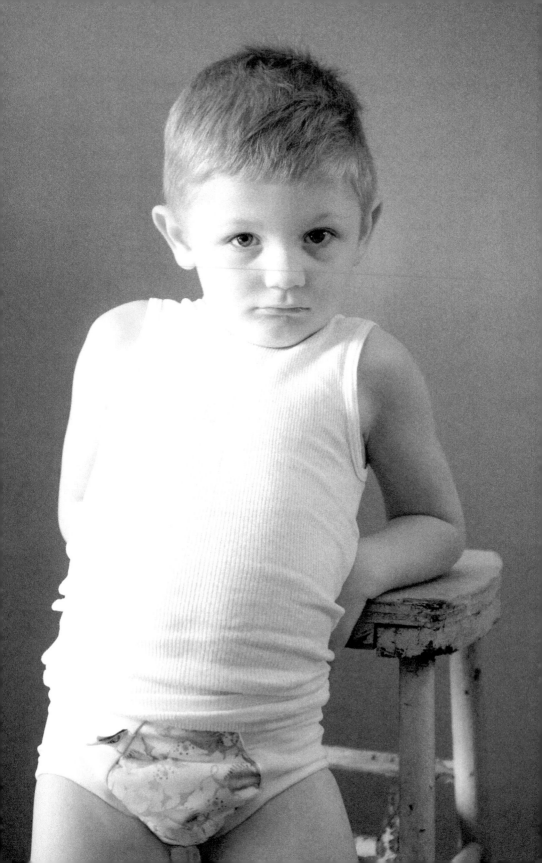

The Compliance Factor

To start our potty training journey, let's just watch for a while. Watching has two critical goals here. You will learn some key characteristics about your child that will help you potty train effectively and you will convince yourself of the fact that your child is ready. Conviction that your child is capable of the task is absolutely necessary and for most people I talk to, it is the greatest contributing factor to potty training anxiety. They just aren't sure that now is the right time.

Now, I'll ask you a question and watch your child for the answer. I encourage you to not just think about this answer and come to a conclusion, but really take a few hours and watch your child's behavior with this question in mind: Does your child listen and follow parental directions consistently?

Why do I say "parental directions" instead of "your directions?" Because in many home environments, I find that a child is trained to deal with each parent differently. They may listen consistently to Dad but whine a lot to Mom, even if they do eventually comply. But what I find even more common is that the primary caretaker, typically Mom, has far more control over the child and the secondary caretaker, often Dad, is labeled as the fun one—the one with no rules.

This simply comes from a reality of Mom being the source of the structure of the home for the majority of the time and Dad swooping in after work to have fun with his kids! Whoever has less time with the children feels more obligated to relax rules and structure and to bond with the kids. I get it and in a way, I can condone that. But in the season of potty training, it's important for both parents to be on the same page and agree on a steady and consistent system for potty training. In short, I want you to talk about this with each other long before you start. If there are two parents in the house, you need to be a unified team so your child is exposed to consistent practices and thus a predictable experience, in his potty training career.

> *"In the season of potty training, it's important for both parents to be on the same page."*

Now, you direct your child constantly through the situations of life: when it's time to take baths, eat lunch, nap time, etc. And for the most part, you may have a compliant child, but what we are about to ask our kids to do is something out of the norm. Long before we potty train, I want you to test your child's compliance level off the potty training playing field. I encourage you to take a week or two and systematically apply the following routine-altering techniques to your toddler's life. The point of this exercise is not only to see if your child is generally obedient, but also to teach obedience and establish who is ultimately in charge.

Remember though, in this mini-program, we are not bargaining. If you always tell your child their choice comes after your choice, you will be instilling in them the idea that life is a give and take, and you can barter for anything. Life often is, but in the early years of life, it is not. You want to show your children that they can trust what you say. They don't need to be in charge because you are competent and they are safe and loved. It is so much work to fight and have to get your own way all the time. Successfully teaching your child to listen the first time will lead to a calmer toddlerhood and an easier potty training experience. Compliance can be broken down into one simple word: Trust. Say it often to your child. Trust me. Mother knows best.

You have four places to hit in life in order to alter your toddler's routine and test/teach compliance while building trust:

- What to eat.
- What to watch on TV.
- What to wear.
- What to play with.

What to Eat

You might think your kid listens to you all the time about what to eat, but the truth also may be that you only give him what he's used to. If you've got a mac n' cheese lover who gets a lot of mac n' cheese, then that isn't effectively testing compliance. Take one week and set a menu.

Children eat smaller amounts often, so think about your menu in terms of a child. It should include breakfast, snack, lunch, snack, dinner, and maybe another snack before bed.

Vary your foods relatively widely and only put common foods on the menu half the time. Stay away from processed foods, which are designed to hit triggers in us that satisfy our desire for salty, fatty, and sweet items, making our kids crave them more and reject fresh foods that can't mimic these triggers. Your child will be free not to eat what they don't want, but do not offer other alternatives. Remember, if you've set the menu to be healthy and tasty, there is no reason that you should be fighting with a child over what they will and will not eat. If you find yourself in this battle, there is an imbalance of authority in the home that will cause problems when attempting to potty train.

Some good, fresh foods that a child may or may not be inclined to try on their own are hummus, black olives, red peppers, carrot sticks, celery sticks, kefir, string cheese, plain rice, wheat berries, quinoa, toast with butter, eggs, and cucumber sticks. Offer new snack combinations, as well! Graham crackers and milk, raisins in oatmeal, bananas or apples with peanut butter—these are good, tasty additions to supplement a fresh menu and by combining foods, you will create new flavors for your child.

Be creative. Use colors and keep it fun. Make it a point to sit with your toddler and eat the same foods with them. Demonstration and leading by example is going to be key in your potty training future. One other way to craft an open mind for your toddler is to talk about the new foods you are eating. Point out how the celery is so crunchy. Then, point out how the carrot is so crunchy and then talk about how the banana is not crunchy; it's soft. If your kid doesn't want to try new foods, you will pique his curiosity about these new attributes the more you talk about them and you may even be teaching him something new! Test this later by putting crunchy and soft foods on a plate and ask your kid to tell you which is crunchy. Correct him if he's wrong and reteach the concepts through food. I want you to see how many times you need to teach something before he can correctly answer. If he picks these things up quickly, it will help convince you of his ability to learn to use the toilet.

After a solid week of menu alterations, you have now successfully taught your child to trust you in new things. You're not feeding him junk and he had fun sitting with you, sharing and learning through every meal.

What to Watch

If you have a cartoon buff on your hands, make sure you begin to vary your television menu with non-animated shows. Some wonderfully fascinating programs are found in nature documentaries, but Planet and Life are both series that offer a wide variety of colors, animals, and scenery. Your child may not agree at first, but don't let her change the channel. Put on what you want her to watch and make sure it stays on, or it will be turned off. If she tries to change the show, tell her two to three times that you are choosing this show and that you will shut off the TV if she continues to change it. Then, follow through.

Not every show needs to be dictated by you, but her TV time should be varied between your choices and hers. Do not get into a place where you are making deals. During most days of the week, in this time of teaching compliance, you should be deciding the TV programs - 100%. Throw their favorite shows in your TV plan, as well, so they see you know what they like, which will help you teach them to trust you. Start out by making a list of all their shows and during the first two days, you can play one to two shows that they like and then throw in a third, new, and different one. The next day, it should be one show they like and know, then a second they don't know. The third day should start off with something completely new. By the end of the week, your TV choices should be at your whim, as you look to entertain and enrich your child's knowledge of the world outside his home.

What to Wear

I remember a time when my second child was two years old and we were heading out to the department store. He insisted on dressing himself and emerged from his room in adorable inappropriateness! It wasn't anything bad, but on our ninety degree summer day, he chose to don super-cute rain galoshes. I told him that it would be too hot to wear those and he told me he loved them and that he was going to wear them. "But they will be hot and you'll be uncomfortable," I said. "No they won't!" he said.

I gave in and we headed out. He wore those things all day until my husband got home. When he asked how long he'd had those galoshes on, I told him and then he scolded me. I had told myself I was allowing a life experience to teach my son what it meant to be "hot" so he could make a more appropriate decision in the future. The real truth, though, is that my son was still learning the basics of how to get along in life. He didn't even know his ABCs yet and I was letting him suffer in the heat, thinking he could learn not to wear them again.

Well, what I really taught him was that if he wanted to wear rainbow galoshes every day of the week, it was his right and he continued trying to exercise that right, rather than learning from our previous day. I had a fight on my hands, knowing that my husband disapproved of my reasoning.

And he was righ t. A two-year-old does not have the capacity to think about his own well-being through the hours of a day and consider heat as a factor to his comfort and well-being. Think about all of those aspects in just that one choice. Leave that kind of decision-making to a child who has had sufficient life experience under wise guidance. That is our job right now, to not empower them in the overwhelming world of making your own choices and all the repercussions of those choices, but to first teach them basics—principles of life they can just learn without question.

Go to the closet or drawers with your toddler and plan out outfits together for the next few days.

Be very talkative about your choices and ask lots of questions, but make sure you get some clothing items in there that are solely your choice and some that are solely their choice. You can hang the outfits in order, leave them laid out on the floor, or set them one on top of the other on the bed or dresser. Each morning, go to the stack with your toddler and get the next outfit you both agreed on. At some point during the week, I want you to suddenly change one of the outfits, but the change has to be your decision solely.

The point of this exercise is twofold. We are demonstrating how to set a plan (like the menu plan) and how to follow it. We are also going to demonstrate that a parent can override any plan, with no questions asked. Again, this gives you the opportunity to see if your kid fully trusts your judgment and will listen. But feel free to have fun with it! Maybe you switch out the chosen outfit with a costume! We want our children to feel safe and trust our choices.

What to Play With

Most of our children are entitled beyond reason. It's true! Children in Africa find complete satisfaction in playing with a ball and a stick for the majority of their games. They don't feel badly for themselves that they don't have the entire Little People playset, complete with the mini jungle gym. Their satisfaction comes in the form of community and games.

My most delightful exercise comes in the form of taking all the toys away from my toddler and making a clean sweep of their room. I am not a terrible, mean monster, but I saw firsthand my children's delight when I taught them this lesson and of course, I delight in their happiness.

Begin by determining where you can put all the stuff. You can use a garage, a shed, the upper shelves of a linen closet, the top shelf of your closet, or wherever you can store the items. Be able to see the toys clearly and limit your child's access to them. Organize the toys by type or play style. Some categories might be playsets, cars, action figures, arts and crafts, education, and imagination play or dress-up. Use this opportunity to clean the toys, throw away anything that is broken, or donate what you want to. A wise person once told me that donating something was giving it to God. She said God knows of a home that could really use it more than I could. Give it to Him and let Him give it to someone else. This makes decluttering much easier for me!

Put all the toys away in the place you've chosen and clean the room well. Take between one and three chosen toys down and let your child back in the room. A child that walks into a clean room with only a few toys sees it as a blank canvas! I've seen time and time again when children become excited about old things. Old becomes new again! They actually forget about most of their toys because there is too much around them to focus on one thing. Rotate the toys every day and each morning becomes like Christmas!

They wake up to something new. When you're choosing your toys, think about the brain functions that the different toys stimulate. One day could be an art day, one day a train table day, another might be teddy bear day, one day is fort building, and another could be moon sand day. You can also rotate toys during nap time.

I know all this may seem arbitrary or trivial, but believe me, if you do this right you will have a child who trusts you and listens. There is a Polish proverb that says, "When you stare at the horse, he wins." Maybe a bit is lost in translation, but it means that whatever you are focusing on will succeed. If it is important to you that you are established as the lead in your home over the children and they listen to you, then this will happen. So many problems will be avoided in the future!

And did you know that you aren't the only one who is afraid to potty train? Some kids develop a fear of elimination and start to hide to poop. Some flat out refuse to poop without a diaper! If your child trusts you and knows fully that you are on their side, then you can help them overcome their fears through solid reassurance. These methods help you establish that line of trust by proving to them that your choices are fun, you're not mean, you love them, and letting you be in control is a safe place for them.

"If your child trusts you and knows fully that"

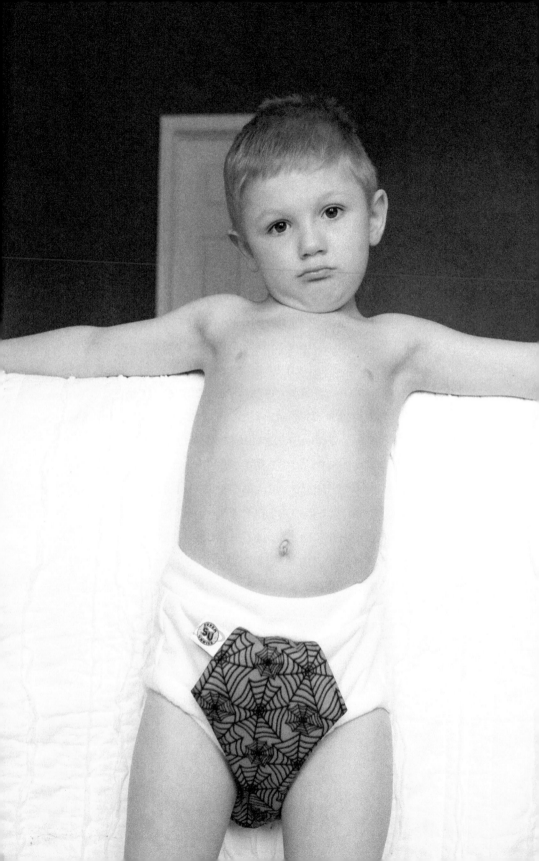

The Fight

If you found some of the compliance tests to be tough, there could be an imbalance of authority in your home. It's very common! Without us even realizing it, these things sneak into our lives and before we know it, we've just accepted it as normal. The only way to set it all straight is to reestablish the hierarchy of the household in the lives of your children and that inevitably results in a fight. Or many fights, but I hope not. When I say "fight," I'm not talking about an all-out brawl. I'm talking about a kid trying to control something he shouldn't be authorized to and a parent taking that power back and putting it where it belongs.

Learning to anticipate and tackle a fight (and win) should be a part of any parent's career. A fight can break out for any number of reasons. Maybe your child just wants something sweet and you're not budging. Maybe he's so used to watching the same show that he doesn't want to watch anything else. Whatever the fight is, don't give in. Your child has two choices: trust you and listen or don't participate.

If he fights over the TV, then shut it off. If he fights over the food, there will be another meal and by that time, he will be hungrier. Just sit down, eat yours, and welcome them to join you. Don't overdo it, though. A kid can tell when we are trying to manipulate them and they learn to apply the same tactics on us. Any manipulation on our part has to be subtle. If they don't eat this meal, clean up your plate, and leave the invitation open for them. These are the two main areas in which you may find yourself in a fight. If you stay firm, calm, and hold your ground, they will eventually tire out. In every fight you find yourself in, just think of how much you love them. This will help remind you why you're in this tough place. It is for their own good.

Let's look at your benefits versus theirs, when starting a fight.

Parents - You can anticipate when a battle will break out and mentally prepare.

Toddler - They plan on getting what they want and crying until they do.

Parents - You can instigate a battle to catch them off guard. Sound mean? It's better than having a three-year-old king ruling the domain!

Toddler - They have "staying power" and lots of practice in this area if they have been ruling the roost.

Parents - They don't know that you're on to them!

A younger child won't typically go through these fights. They are still in learning mode and are generally accepting of parents introducing new things. Toddlers over two, most commonly two-and-a-half and up, are most likely to demand their own way. It is natural for a child to test the levels of independence granted to them.

When my first child was about twenty-four months old, he cried and whined for everything. I taught him this behavior completely unintentionally. I was so afraid of a meltdown, that I had a really hard time saying "no." It got to the point where he would ask for a cookie (or tell me to give him one) and I would! Because if I didn't, he would cry. Oh, poor me! I would have to deal with a crying kid. I was young and I didn't know what kind of monster could be bred from this type of entitled environment. But eventually, I realized things were out of control. I was out of control. I was frustrated with my own son and I wasn't enjoying life as a mom at all.

> *"In every fight you find yourself in, just think of how much you love them. This will help remind you why you're in this tough place. It is for their own good."*

There is one particular morning I remember well. The sun was shining. We slept in till 10 a.m. I was well-rested. My kitchen was clean. I remember feeling particularly calm and peaceful this morning, still getting used to the fact that all I had to do in life was stay at home with my baby. It was my job to raise this kid and make him into someone great. That's all I had to do. Then, The Boy woke up.

He came into the kitchen and looked around. He spotted a bag of Oreos on the counter and pointed.

"Coo-kie?" He said in his cute little person voice.

"No, not now," I said. I couldn't believe I said "no." I knew what was coming and braced myself.

"Coo-kie?!" he said again, a bit louder.

"No, not for breakfast," I said again, cringing inside.

And then it started. That whining that is just the perfect pitch to make your skin crawl and pierce your brain. I hated it! I tried to ignore it, but he persisted. Now he was at full volume, screaming for the cookie. I had no clue what to do! I was across the country from any family members that could have guided my young soul in matters of temper tantrums. I just stood there, turned my back to him, and plugged my ears. How juvenile, I know! He went on and on and was now rolling on the floor. After about four minutes of sheer noise abuse, I snapped. I swung around and at the top of my lungs I screamed at him, "STOOOOOP IIIIIIIIT!"

He was stunned, quiet, then began to cry for real. A sad, quieter cry. I had never screamed at the top of my lungs before, let alone screamed at someone - let alone someone I loved! Thoughts flashed through my mind. If anyone knew I screamed like that at my baby, they would call the cops or Child Protective Services! I went down on my knees and was acutely aware of how bad my throat hurt. I felt SO bad. I put my arms out to him and he waddled over to me. I just hugged him and we both cried.

I realized I no longer had control of my home because I didn't have control over my child. My husband had been growing frustrated with our home life and I didn't know why, until now. Unfortunately, he was powerless to make any real changes in our home because he was always at work. All he could do was passive-aggressively show me his disappointment about how things were playing out.

After much reflection, I was bent on getting things straightened out. This kid would not, could not, own me anymore. I was failing at my job! My job wasn't to raise him and give him whatever he wanted. It was to make him into a great person. I wasn't setting him up with realistic expectations of the world. He was completely convinced that he was the only thing on the planet that needed to be tended to and I was his servant. That's when I hatched my plan to set things straight.

I decided I would catch The Boy off guard and outmaneuver him. I went and bought a pack of Oreos and put them on top of the refrigerator. I knew the little cookie monster would see them and I was right. When he woke up the next morning, he came out to the kitchen and saw them. He pointed up and asked super sweetly for a cookie. I said "no." He asked again and I said "no" again. Well, progressively he went from a sweet kid to crying and throwing himself on the floor, again. I calmly put one earbud in my ear, listened to some good music, and sat at the sewing machine. This was my therapy. I was in his line of sight, so he could see me completely not caring that he was crying and attempting to dent the floor with his kicking. I stayed focused on not sewing my fingers, which helped take my mind off of something that would normally tear me apart inside.

He screamed for forty-five minutes. I timed it. Every time he caught me looking at him, he would start up louder. I am not telling you to not give attention to the tantrum. Give attention as you see fit to let your child know you are still there, but that you refuse to engage on this level. You don't have to separate him, but you do need to have a plan to occupy your mind. Knitting, crocheting, listening to an audiobook, coloring, working on a spreadsheet, answering emails, going on Facebook, doing laundry—whatever is needed to help you switch your focus. By staying present with him and not reacting to the mess, you will be teaching your child that you meant what you said, but that he is safe. Locking him in a room during a temper tantrum won't help build the trust you are trying to establish at this point in his life. When I say "stay present," I am not referring to staying at his side. Be in sight and occasionally go to him, pat his back, and tell him he can stop any time. Then, go back to what you were doing.

I told him he could eat a cookie after lunch, so he ate breakfast (finally) and asked for a cookie. I told him, "No, after lunch." He proceeded to cry and whine for twenty-six minutes (I timed it again). I didn't need to sew this time. I was so ready for this. I was excited to win! He cooled off and ended up playing with toys. Then, we had lunch and he asked for a cookie. He got it.

The next morning, he woke up, came into the kitchen, saw the cookies, and asked for one again. He went into meltdown mode quickly when he heard the answer and proceeded to throw a fit. This one lasted ten minutes. He just eventually got up and went to play. I was ecstatic. I won! I took my power back from the two-year-old! Victory dance!!

As time progressed and my little sugar addict continued to ask for cookies, he understood my answer and went away without a fight. Three times. We had three good fights and I won them all. They were close together and he learned to listen to me. Things got easier in life. I noticed that when I used the same tone as saying "no" for the cookie (which was matter-of-fact, because I meant it), he didn't fight me. If I used a more wishy-washy tone on something, he tried harder to get his way. A child's brain at this age is primed for learning. They are soaking up, internalizing, and incorporating every experience into their lives so quickly that we would be amazed! They are built for learning and growing. We need to teach them well, set good examples, and stifle bad habits quickly.

The main point of all of this is learning how to win a fight outside of the potty training arena. If you don't have a toddler that is obedient, you're going to have a hard time potty training. Fight the fight off the potty training playing field and you'll have a much easier time potty training.

> *"We had three good fights and I won them all. They were close together and he learned to listen to me."*

The Stubborn Children

I say "stubborn" because that is how many parents describe their toddlers to me, but I really think we should alter the way we think about this inclination to be more independent. Independence and confidence are highly sought-after characteristics in older children and adults, but they do pose challenges for parents raising these spirited children. Just remind yourself of how amazing they can be in the future. However, as parents, we need to be mindful and teach these kids the right paths to walk so we do not create a defiant streak. An independent streak is certainly something that every child will go through, and naturally so. If your child is highly independent, it is important for them to be able to make some decisions about their life. Determine where you will give them this independence before you ever engage in a battle for the home.

Independent children can really thrive when given important jobs to do. They will feel valued and appreciated, which will help curb their need to control things later on. Teaching a toddler to sweep a floor, wash the mirrors, or wipe the kitchen cabinets can help them feel valued and older, since you are letting them do adult jobs. Don't worry if the work isn't perfect, of course. Just make sure your independent child feels important and valued in the home.

If the idea of implementing the four ways to test and teach compliance makes you cringe or causes dread thinking about the fights that may ensue, then roll out the program over a longer period of time. Take one week for each exercise. A gradual change, along with giving your child valued jobs in the house, will help ease them into the transition of you being in charge.

Getting Your Way and Avoiding the Fight

The best tool you have on your side in potty training your kid could quite simply be changing how you speak to him. So many times, I've seen moms turn to their kids after talking to me and say to their two- or three-year-old, "Are you ready to potty train? Mommy wants to start potty training. Are you ready?"

I just chuckle to myself. No, he isn't ready. He didn't just sit through a forty-five-minute lecture taking notes, growing, and getting ready to get the job done. He didn't just privately seek counsel from me about his fears and what to watch out for. He isn't ready. Then, the kid replies, "No!" Of course, he said that.

We need to learn that a question implies a choice. Tell, don't ask. The best way to get proven results in toddlers is to get down on their level, eye to eye, and tell them what you want them to do. Save asking questions for things like, "Are you hot?" or "Are you hungry?" If your questions always start with, "Do you want," then you just made them ruler over the situation. Too many of these questions and they place themselves as ruler over the family. Even the question, "Do you have to go potty?" can get a negative response, because they don't know what that feels like yet. Just ask them to sit on the toilet, relax, and try to see if something will come out.

Remember, Mother knows best. In fact, Father knows best, too. You know what they need to eat to be healthy, how they should be playing to grow best, how fresh air is essential to a growing brain, and after reading this book, you will know how to potty train, not them. So, let them go along for the ride, but you steer the ship.

"The best way to get proven results in toddlers is to get down on their level, eye to eye, and tell them what you want them to do."

You would be shocked at the statement I got from my seven-year-old daughter after we brawled it out. She wanted her way and wasn't going to get it. After a while, she went into full-on tantrum mode and thrashed her room. She tore her bed clothes off her bed and threw her stuffed animals all over. She swiped books off their shelves. She had a good old-fashioned rock star hotel room thrashing! I'd never seen a kid do this before, but she always has been my creative one. I stayed calm, stood my ground, and gave her space. After she had been done crying, I told her she gets to clean it all up now. Another meltdown ensued! It took her an hour and a half with mini meltdowns in between, but eventually, she was done. When it was all over, I had her take a shower to wash away all the tears and emotions and cool her down. She came downstairs all clean and gave me the biggest hug. She said, "Thank you Mommy."

"For what?" I asked.

"For making sure I did what I needed to. For helping get the bad out of me."

"So, you're happy that I disciplined you?" I asked.

"Yes," she said.

She told me her brain was just all crazy and she was so focused on getting her way. She told me how angry she was at me and how she doesn't want to be like that. I was so touched. She affirmed so much for me that day. That wasn't the first time one of my children thanked me for disciplining them and pulling them out of their madness. It was just the most recent time. Kids don't want to be mean. They don't want to cry all the time and they don't want to throw tantrums. They really do crave structure and it's an easier life to let someone else be in control. They just need someone to help them learn that.

From Jill Y.

Two questions—My three-, almost four-year-old, throws lots of fits when he doesn't get his way…proceeds to strip. Then pee all over the floor/bed. Sometimes pees in his clothes also. I've stopped calling them accidents because I believe he does it on purpose…I call it his angry pees. When he does this, I make him help clean it up, and he loses TV that night. Any advice?

Also, my 18-month-old has been going on the potty on and off for a couple months now; sometimes he refuses to put a diaper on! Should I be forcing him to wear a diaper when leaving the house/ nap…or just deal with the mess if he has accidents?

Dear Jill,

You are right on! This is a shift from potty training to parenting. If you believe he is doing this on purpose, he probably is. No one knows him better than you. If he has to clean it up and loses TV, then just stay this course. If it doesn't change in a few days, change your tactic. He will need to lose something else, and you will just have to find his currency.

I knew a woman whose daughter was having "fake accidents," and Mom told her she wasn't able to go out of the house until they stopped. "You can't pee in a store, and we can't trust that you won't." The first day, the family went out for fast food, but Mom and her daughter stayed home. The next day, the family left them and went to Chuck E. Cheese's. They strategically went places the daughter would like to go, and by the third day, the daughter was magically accident-free! Hope this helps!

The Sticky On Poop
Young potty trainers

Yes, poop. It will come up at some point in this process. The earlier you introduce the toilet, the better. This gives your child a lot less time to develop anxiety over this. Yup, kids can have a terrible amount of anxiety for a variety of reasons here. First, though, I want to tell you a story about my experience with my eight-month-old pooping in the potty. Yes, I said that correctly. No, we weren't doing elimination communication.

I was at a holistic parents meetup group, just beginning to explore healthy options for my family and I met a woman from Belarus. She had an eleven-month-old with her. As we mingled and talked about all things baby, she revealed to me that she was surprised to see how long children stayed in diapers here in the U.S. She then went on to tell me that her son poops on the potty all the time and never in his diaper. Of course, I had to know how, so here is what she said:

It is common in Russia to begin training your children to use the "pot" early on. It used to be an actual pot they put on the floor and when the baby woke up, the baby was put on the pot until he eliminated. Parents typically start this around six months old. In her case, she transferred this behavior to the standard toilet. Every morning, she took her newly awake baby to the toilet and sat him on the front of it, then pulled him forward. This may sound uncomfortable, but it is not at all. The baby sits there, collapsed toward the front and you just hold onto them at their sides. Feel free to let your baby lean into you, as well!

Babies don't fight and struggle as toddlers do. They pretty much hang out where you put them. Since babies naturally eliminate as they wake up (or just after), it becomes very easy to catch some potty action like this!

That's it. That is how she started. She added that as her baby pooped in the toilet, she would make a sound to help him correlate the two. Like language. She was naming the action with a sound. Within a week, she could then put her baby on the toilet, make this sound (i.e., tell him to poop), and he would release his bowels. No more crappy diapers. This just sounded too good to be true! My son was eight months old at the time and I was game to give this method a shot!

The next morning, I wanted to try, but I was too late. When I heard him wake up, I went to put him on the toilet, but he had already gone in his diaper. I wasn't attentive enough to the prewake- up phase of babyhood, I suppose.

However, the next morning I was ready! I listened intently for his little noises that meant he was in the process of waking up. I gently picked him up and talked to him. Then, I took him to the potty, sat him on the edge of the toilet, and pulled him forward. We sat there for a few minutes. Within the first minute, he peed! I was super excited and almost whisked him off to find the phone and call Grandma, but then I came back to my senses. There could be more.

Somewhere around the third or fourth minute, my eight-month-old pooped on the toilet. I just couldn't believe it! This unheard of, surreal phenomenon actually took place in my bathroom!

This truly opened my eyes to the capabilities of our children. Perhaps they are smarter than we give them credit for. Maybe we can control more than we think. I began experimenting with other times to put him on the toilet and discovered that we didn't even need to add in a sound for him to know what to do. Later that same day, after lunch, he peed on the toilet. No cues, just mommy hunches that it would be about time for him to go. We caught a few pees on the potty, changed another poopy diaper, took note of the time he pooped, and went to bed. The next morning, he pooped and peed again on the toilet, this time more quickly. Remember, within just twenty-four hours, this little guy now had six experiences with using the toilet and his little brain, which is perfectly primed and optimized for learning, was doing its job!

I have heard so many perspectives on the readiness of potty training, whether you look for signs of readiness in your child or take on a parent-led approach. I just want to encourage mothers out there that potty training is not a big deal when you are working with a child that is not so complicated. As a child gets older, we end up adding in the influence of television, impacts of play dates and friends, diets laced with sugar, bribes for expected behavior, and busy schedules.

Now, we might find toilet training to be a more difficult creature in life. We now have to navigate who our children are becoming through these influences, as well as appease their newly eveloping independent streak.

But, I do want to finish my story. I want to be very clear here. I did not have a potty-trained baby. It was never my goal. I simply hated changing dirty diapers. There, I said it. I absolutely hated it. I also hate laundry. I did then and I do now. Oh, and I'm really cheap. See? I have a few things stacked against me in this quest that crashed upon me to become some domestic goddess. Getting my baby to poop in the toilet meant I had less laundry to do from any bowel movement blowout (you know what I'm talking about). It saved me from having a huge load of cloth diapers, saved me from having to use another disposable diaper (we were half and half), saved me from having to change a poopy diaper on a five-hour flight, and saved me money.

My husband recognized this developed behavior as "Pavlovian." He told me about Pavlov's dogs, which made me cringe at first, thinking there was some animal training involved here, but this experiment translates perfectly to humans, as well.

Ivan Pavlov was the founder of what we currently know as "classical conditioning." Classical conditioning refers to an involuntary biological response brought about by an external stimulus.

A classic example is how you begin salivating when you smell food. Pavlov proved classical conditioning in an experiment where he first rang a bell and then he would feed his dogs.

Eventually, the dogs would begin to salivate when they heard the bell, even if there was no food present. It proved a mental link between our biological responses and an environment. He went on with more experiments that tested the same theory.

What was happening with my son was the same Pavlovian response. We didn't know we were developing it, but it did result nonetheless. My son did not necessarily hold his pee or poop until we sat on the potty. He did still wear a diaper and I was free to change it or not. He did not argue or make any fuss when wet; he was not aware at that level. He was eight months old. But, sitting him on the potty did elicit an elimination response in him every time. If there was something in there, it would come out. If there wasn't, we knew in the first few moments.

One thing I can certainly attest to, though, is that this incredible familiarity with the toilet completely skirted any odd poop anxiety we could have had. The toilet had become a common tool in the house and pooping in it just wasn't a big deal. When my son turned two, we were using about four diapers a day and they were all wet. I decided to potty train at that point and began explaining what he would have to do. We said we would start Monday and that he would not have a diaper anymore after that point. Since he was so familiar with the toilet already, he was truly potty trained in two days. If you have a young child, you don't need to start potty training, but you certainly should be trying to make some potty time a natural behavior in the house.

Older potty trainers

At this point in life, you have probably already dabbled in potty training. Perhaps you have tried, met resistance, and took a few steps back. Maybe you haven't tried anything, not being entirely sure if your child is ready. For whatever reason, you have found yourself with an older child who is not potty trained. Unfortunately, this is where the majority of pooping and potty training issues begin, but don't worry, we'll be tackling them.

The most common problems parents will face with older potty trainers are:

- Hiding to poop.
- Refusing to poop without a diaper on, even if they pee in the potty.
- Poop withholding or refusing to poop at all.
- Only pooping when at home.

If you already have some of these issues, don't just jump into potty training! What I'm going to lay out here is a way to avoid many of these problems and potentially undo them.

Just about all major poop-related issues are rooted in one of three things:

- Allergy.
- Fear.
- Entitlement.

Allergy

A parent can usually tell if this frustrating issue is due to an allergy. Signs of this include runny stools, a child not knowing they have to poop or being caught off guard when pooping, and painful stools. To get a good sense on whether or not your child's stools are normal, check out the Bristol Stool Chart to determine which stool your child has. If the stool does not have the proper consistency, then the child will not have the necessary sensation that gives us time to get to the toilet. If you suspect an allergy, please see your family physician. It is very challenging and frustrating for both parent and child to attempt to potty train when your little one doesn't have the right sensations happening to be successful. It's like setting them up for failure.

Once an allergy is ruled out, now we start the hard work. Fear or entitlement. Most parents don't want to think about either of these options, but this truly does hold the key to your success.

Bristol Stool Chart
Adapted from the Bristol Stool Scale

Type 1		Separate harder lumps, (hard to pass)	Very Constipated
Type 2		Sausage-shaped, lumpy not smooth	Constipated
Type 3		Sausage-shaped but with cracks on its surface	Normal ✓
Type 4		Like a rope, smooth and soft	Normal ✓
Type 5		Soft blobs with clear cut edges (passed easily)	Lacks Fiber
Type 6		Fluffy or mushy stool	Imflamation
Type 7		Watery, no solid pieces	Inflamation

From Stephanie V.

My 17-month-old peed on the potty today for the first time. I honestly thought it was going to be another "tricked you" moment where he sits on the potty for a few moments, gets up, and runs to another room and pees on the floor after his shower/bath.

Our dilemma: He is non-verbal and gets signs mixed up all the time (e.g., signs "more" when he wants milk or "all done" when he wants to eat and is never consistent using the same signs for anything). He also has FPIES [Food Protein-Induced Enterocolitis Syndrome], which has limited his diet and caused food aversions, so giving him food/candy is not an option to praise him. He hates stickers and will rip/bite them in half and throw them away, so that's out the door for praising him. On top of it, he has kidney issues, and his urologist suggested holding off until after he is 2 to potty train. We only got the potty to introduce it to him, as he had become so intrigued by Mommy/Daddy using the potty to the point of trying to wipe and flushing the potty for us. We will be moving in a little over a month.

Current situation: He hides in the bathroom to poop unless he is having a reaction due to his FPIES. He will pinch/tug at his diaper if he has peed in it and will go hysterical if he even feels damp. He has never liked sitting on his potty with the diaper, only will if he is without his diaper and pants. Every time me or my husband go to the bathroom, our kiddo is nipping at our heels and has us take his diaper off so he can sit on the potty, too. When he wakes up from a nap, he usually pouts after he has peed in his diaper and then wants to sit on the potty before he gets a clean diaper. More often than not, he wakes up in the morning dry despite nursing multiple times at night, but I usually have to change his diaper (especially if he is in cloth) at some point between 3-5 a.m.

So my questions are:

1. Should we continue allowing him to use the potty without expectations since it's been recommended to hold off (I get more information in late January from his urologist)?

2. What are ways to praise him other than saying, "Yay!" or "Good/great job!" or "Oh my goodness, you peed/pooped on the potty. You're such a big boy!"

3. Does moving tend to cause problems with potty training later?

4. And if we continue to allow him to use the potty without expectations, when we are traveling for our move, should we have the potty available when we stop at hotels/family's homes?

Dear Stephanie,

You should certainly hold off on potty training and follow the urologist's advice. However, you are not potty training. He is! So, you should allow him to continue to discover these things as he wishes. Having a portable potty available in the hotel room is completely reasonable. The reason your urologist does not want him to potty train young is because the idea of potty training must include the ability to hold in your poop and urine until an opportunity to release it arises. Once children begin holding back, then they become more susceptible to bladder infections.

I would begin to pay attention to see if he is actually holding his movements until he gets to the toilet, rather than going in his diaper. This is the behavior your urologist wants to avoid. If he is using the potty and going constantly as soon as the urge hits, then there's nothing to worry about and you can safely continue as is.

I would not bring incentives into this yet. That would be full-blown potty training and would teach him more to hold it. Let your son do as he is doing, but let him lead everything until you see your doctor again.

There is a simple formula you can apply to each of these poop-related issues to undo their dastardly ways:

Allergy ————> Family physician
Fear ————> Knowledge and trust
Entitlement ————-> Earned privileges

There, wasn't that easy? That is the short answer to combating the root of these problems.

Although I cannot help you with allergies, I can help you with the other two. This is where a shift in parenting style comes into play. Most fear at a kid's level is rooted in the unknown. Like being afraid of the dark! Even though they are in their room - the place that holds all the greatest toys and awesomeness in their entire world - shut the lights off and they can't see anything. It's unknown. Turn the lights on or give them a nightlight and now they can see. Now, they have knowledge of what's around them. You can undo any irrational fear with the right kind of knowledge and a nice level of trust. Trust is essential in a kid's world because he needs to believe what you say is true. If you are having pooping issues due to fear, it is absolutely necessary to start having many conversations with your kids long before potty training. Let me suggest the topic of "systems."

Every "Body" Has a System

This is ultimately what any anxious or fearful child has to learn, that every "body" has a system.

Knowledge takes away the mystery. Depending on the age of your toddler or child, they will not pick up every piece of information you feed them, but using kid language you certainly can teach them about how everything is connected. And please don't worry. Offering your children information that may be over their head just reinforces that you know more than them. They will be more apt to listen to you about things later on in life.

Show them how the weather has a system. Where something scary like lightning comes from.

How scary sharks are in the ocean, but they eat fish, not people (it's true, they only bite people by mistake and then let them go, but you don't have to include that part). And do you know how important spiders are to our world? Without spiders, we would be overrun with insects! Spiders help to keep things in order around us by eating those insects— then pooping them out. Taking things that are scary and demystifying them with reasonable explanations and pointing to the benefits and necessities of these wonderful critters will get your child ready to accept a whole new world.

Share episodes of *Dirty Jobs with Mike Rowe* with them! This television program shows people how all sorts of things are made and why it's important. There are even some episodes about sewage in there! Take some time to look at how a bee greets a flower. Your kid probably doesn't know about how bees can sting yet, but did you know that a bee will visit a bush and stop at every flower on it, without returning to a flower he already visited? It's remarkable to think about. How does he know where he's been? How can he remember?

Did you know that whales and dolphins can talk to each other? They use high-pitched noises that can travel miles through the water to reach farther out family members, then softer sounds and clicks to speak to those close by.

Did you know that butterflies taste things through sensors in their feet? You will be fostering a love of nature and respect for our planet, as well as prepping them to accept why other people do not wear diapers. By teaching your toddler all these things, you are "telling them" about the world. You're not asking them. If you tell your child about the world, you are ultimately teaching them to accept things they have no control over. You are proving life is bigger than just them. The planet is a great place with unchangeable aspects to it and potty training has unchangeable aspects to it. You can even apply these systems in a more hands-on, practical way.

Let's look at the systems in a house. Every time we eat dinner, someone has to wash the dishes.

Talk about what happens if you didn't. Every morning, we have to wake up and every night, we have to go to sleep. These are things that cannot be changed. It is how life will always be. Talk about what happens if we don't do these things. Every time we put liquid in us, the liquid has to come out and every time we eat, the food will have to come out, as well. It is just something that has to happen - for everyone in any age in any part of the world.

Do this fun demonstration!

Get a water balloon (or any balloon) and show your child how this balloon is like your body. We drink juice and water and milk (fill the balloon up very slowly at the kitchen faucet). Now, stop and show your kid how the water sits in the balloon. This is the liquid inside us. It sits in our stomach and works through our body. It helps the rest of our body to work. But, we can't keep it in there forever! Slowly fill the balloon with more water and stop again. We are NOT going to talk about this balloon bursting. We don't need to scare our kids more and this is not a practical thing that will happen to us. But, we can talk about how we might start feeling sick. Maybe there is pressure in our bladders. Maybe our tummy hurts. This is why we have a second place in us designed to let food and drink back out.

Now, take a second balloon and pop a little hole in the bottom BEFORE putting water in it. Show your kid that this is how our body actually works. Pinch the hole and fill the balloon with water again. Stop and talk about how a person feels full when they eat or drink enough. Then, unpinch the hole and watch the water drain back out. This is an excellent way to explain what's actually happening when we pee and why we need to learn where to put our poop and pee. As long as we are eating and drinking, this cycle will never stop.

I want you to clearly explain why babies wear diapers, as well. Many parents like to continually point out that big kids wear underwear and babies wear diapers. They are using a guilt or shame tactic to try and encourage their children to rise to a new level, but they leave out an important piece of the equation—why babies wear diapers.

Diapers are necessary for babies to wear because they are constantly peeing and pooping with no notice. If Mom was breastfeeding a baby and the baby pooped on her lap, she would have yucky, smelly, brownish-yellow poop all over her. Since poop is never allowed to go back in the body once it is out and since the baby is in the middle of eating, he could accidentally eat some of this poop. That's why parents need to have their children in diapers. It gives the pee and poop a place to go until the baby gets changed. Remember our discussion about germs? Poop germs have to stay in that place and a diaper helps with that goal.

Point out to your toddler how no one ever keeps a poopy diaper on for long. The diaper's only function was to give the poop a place to wait until it could be thrown out or flushed. That is why adults don't need diapers. When a person is big enough to walk to the bathroom himself, he can get his poop right in the toilet and the toilet throws it out for us.

It makes sense, right? Having this kind of conversation with your child will help them turn into thinkers. "Thinking" is actually a globally traded commodity. Every year, America outsources more and more jobs to foreigners because we are not creating enough high-quality thinkers in our country. My husband is a software architect, code monkey, and infrastructures security specialist. He runs a few teams of programmers that build software platforms based on what the business departments ask of them. His job is to design the platform needed and guide developers as they push the limits of modern day technology and known coding techniques. His best asset is truly his mind, but he's really cute too!

However, in his experience with hiring, he does see that China and India are producing more quality thinkers than Americans who come with university degrees. Maybe this stems from a generation of more entitled youth and a culture that rewards children with trophies for participation. Maybe part of this is too many mindless cartoons, mounds of toys, and desires filled as soon as they are realized and not enough family game time and dinners at the dining

room table. And then again, maybe not. I will say no more. This area is not my specialty, but I do hope it encourages you to understand that the next generation counts on you. For our children to be valuable in the future workforce, they are going to have to be thinkers.

So, reread the chapter on compliance and take to heart what they watch on TV. Make a shift from Nickelodeon to documentaries. Make a conscious effort to rat out any source of fast-paced racing in life and replace it with a calmer, home-based learning environment where you shepherd your child's future. Do this at least a few weeks before you ask them to change a vital part of their life forever. Start talking more about trust. It's going to become a significant factor in whether a child is willing to conquer his fear or not. Applying this advice to your parenting style can singlehandedly undo pooping issues by just undoing the fear that surrounds them. Through education and trust building, fear doesn't stand a chance against a parent who wants the best for their young!

Entitlement

It's tough to think of a toddler as entitled, isn't it? In addition to the chapter How Entitlement Affects Potty Training, I'd like to address this topic directly relating to an older kid who refuses to potty train. Hold on to your hats, folks! This could be a bumpy ride!

Entitlement is bred by an imbalance in relationships. The younger (typically) feels elevated above the older. Our children are given everything they need right from the start, but it is common for parents to miss the area where things shift from "need" to "want." When I was a young mom, I was completely focused on raising my son. I didn't have any other direction in life. I just got up and served him from morning to night. On the weekends, I would be bored so we would head "out." Well, that usually meant going to the mall or Toys "R" Us. We would walk through the toy shops and play with anything the little one felt drawn to. When we left, we would buy something. Every. Single. Time. Eventually, I had the good sense to realize that my child was being spoiled rotten. It may have had something to do with the fact that this kid would grab at things in the store and threw a fit when I told him "no." This caused me to break out in an anxious sweat, gasping for air at the thought of grocery shopping with him. I started giving him to his dad when I had to run errands. I thought I ruined the kid! I finally broke down and gave my husband the scoop. I told him it was ridiculous that our son and I couldn't go hang out without spending money! We were blowing through $200 every weekend on eating out and kid crap and we didn't even realize it. We just knew we were broke all the time. So, we made a plan. A dastardly plan that would set things right once and for all! We would go to the stores, have a great time, and buy NOTHING! That's right, nothing. It worked like a charm! We elicited the exact response we expected from our toddler - rage. It didn't start out as rage, of course. Just whining and crying at first, but when the reality of not getting anything set in - rage. The boy screamed and threw a fit until he passed out, while Peter and I did our best to ignore it all. This is an example of extreme entitlement. I admit I was the cause, but these things can be undone in a matter of days. My child was only two at this point, so entitlement may look different in an older child. Here are a few things I've heard parents say that tells me they are dealing with an entitled (and resistant) potty trainer.

My child is potty trained at daycare, but refuses to use the toilet when she comes home.

My child was potty trained for weeks, then one day decided to quit. He has accidents now all the time and acts like he doesn't feel them!

My child used to be potty trained, but now she makes up excuses all the time for not using the toilet any more.

My child is basically potty trained when out, but seems lazy and has accidents at home.

My child is potty trained and doesn't wear diapers, but when she needs to poop she brings me a diaper to put on her, then goes in it and asks to be changed right away.

In many of these cases, parents claim their child is potty trained or was potty trained, but somehow the process is not done. It typically revolves around poop.

Entitlement is the attitude of your child that says, "You can't make me" or "This is how I want to do it." It is them deciding the rules and having you follow them. It can all be undone by having them work for their privileges. Much of what we provide for our children does not fall under the category of "rights." They are privileges. Gifts. Free things my kid can have because I have them or things you can do because they're available to do. So let's talk currency and how to use it.

If you feel manipulated by your toddler and don't know how to get control back, look around you and start to see things as currency. Kids don't operate with money yet. Everything that falls into the "extra" category is like money to a kid. TV, toys, movies, sweets, Legos, bubble baths, rides on toys, fairy wings, and dress up clothes. All these things and more flow freely in our homes and our children don't have to do anything to earn them. If your toddler is manipulating you, it's time for your toddler to "get a job." They get to earn their goodies now.

I'm not suggesting you take everything away. I'm suggesting you zero in on what your child likes the most and hold that item hostage. Wait, that sounds mean. I mean, put that item in your family "store" so your toddler can "rent it." I truly did this. I had some linen closets that were up too high for The Boy to reach, but if I opened the door, he could see. I cleared out all the towels and sheets and set up the shelves with his favorite toys on display. I told him he could have them when he _____. Fill in the blank_____. As you know from just a few of my stories, I had some pretty deep seated parenting faux-pas in my past and this is just one one more way I regained control.

Let's look at some suggestions from people that might get your head wrapped around what could work for you…

Alashandra -

My second son refused to use the toilet, and all the candy and toys in the world wouldn't motivate him. When little-tyke wrestling season was coming up, I told him he couldn't join unless he was potty trained. Three days later he was a pro!

Tracy -

My child is a poop holder. He was holding it Saturday morning, and I knew he needed to go. I told him he had to go poop before he could have a cupcake at his birthday party.

That kid sat and pooped for over 20 minutes, then asked for his cupcake!

Jeanette -

My son once caught me having a scoop of ice-cream right out of the carton in the freezer.

He wanted one too, so I told him it was my reward for pooping in the potty. When he pooped in the potty, he could have one. Like magic people! He went, and we've never looked back!

Chelsea -

I hit a wall. My three year old refused to poop in the potty, even though she had been potty trained for almost a year. She just refused. I don't think she was scared, I just think she really didn't want to. I finally just shut off the TV and told her, "you can watch it again when you poop in the toilet. It's not that big a deal. There's nothing to be afraid of.

Let me know when you do and I'll turn the TV back on again." By the end of the day, she was potty trained.

Laurie -

The Lego Mini Figure... My son was hopelessly enthralled by these little guys. He had one clutched in his fist wherever he went! When it was time to learn to poop in the potty, I decided he could earn these little guys. I swooped them all up while he slept, then told him he could have them back for the whole day when he pooped on the potty. It worked!

The majority of these stories show how clever parents manipulated their current situation and caused the child to work for what this kid thought he would get anyway. TV? Kids always get to watch TV! Not anymore, mister! I give extra props to the mom who used her son's birthday cupcake as ransom for getting the boy to do what she KNEW he could do. The question on the other end of this scenario becomes this - Would she still have let him have his birthday cupcake, even if he didn't go to the bathroom? Watch what your response is! The only acceptable answer is NO! If you say it, you MUST follow through with it! Many parents just aren't at this level of commitment until they "hit the wall." There's nowhere else to go and you've tried everything. So yes, one birthday cupcake isn't going to traumatize the kid for life, but it is going to establish your word as something far more substantial than it's ever been! A cupcake is easy enough to make the next day (or even the next week!). Follow through, friends. Don't give up.

Say something tough, then stick with it. If your little one cries, just know this is the process of them working out what they are now responsible to do. No one can MAKE them poop in the potty. Be kind, but follow through and you'll have a kid who figures it out.

Wiping

You can't get away from this subject, but it is often overlooked and underclarified. You MUST teach your children proper wiping habits, hopefully before potty training. You can even have them practice this skill fully clothed, as a preparatory activity. It will help to create interest in your child about what this "potty training" thing is you keep talking about.

Teach that wiping always happens from front to back. Tell them that the yuckies need to be in the toilet and not get on other parts of you, which can happen if you are wiping to the front. Practice while sitting on the couch or a chair and show them how you can lift up one cheek to help gain access to your wipeable bits and pieces. Have them practice and check out their form. Now is the time to make any corrections! But, assure your child that you will always be able to wipe them after they do, just to make sure they are clean.

Parents often want to know how long it will take for a kid to be fully independent with wiping.

Plan on helping your little one for a while! Kids can usually master this skill between the ages of three and four. Charmin makes flushable wet wipes that come in a tub to help kids get clean.

Since their skills are still subpar at this point, it is an excellent idea to give them any advantage you can!

When a child isn't getting clean enough, it is common for a slightly painful or itchy red irritation to form in the ... butt crack. Not sure what the technical term is for this area, but let's call it the crack. There is an easy way to handle this and reduce irritation in just a few short hours. Head your tyke to the bathroom, de-pants them, and ask them to touch their toes. This will expose the crack, so you can see how bad it is. Wet a cotton ball with witch hazel and clean the area. Wet a second cotton ball and hold it in their crack with one finger. Then, ask your child to stand up. This will trap the cotton ball in the crack! Kids usually giggle and think it's funny. It will help sooth them and lessen the irritation. Next time you go potty, the cotton ball can just fall in the toilet and get flushed. Don't worry about your kid feeling the cotton ball and being uncomfortable. They only notice it in the beginning. Then, the feeling fades and it's life as usual.

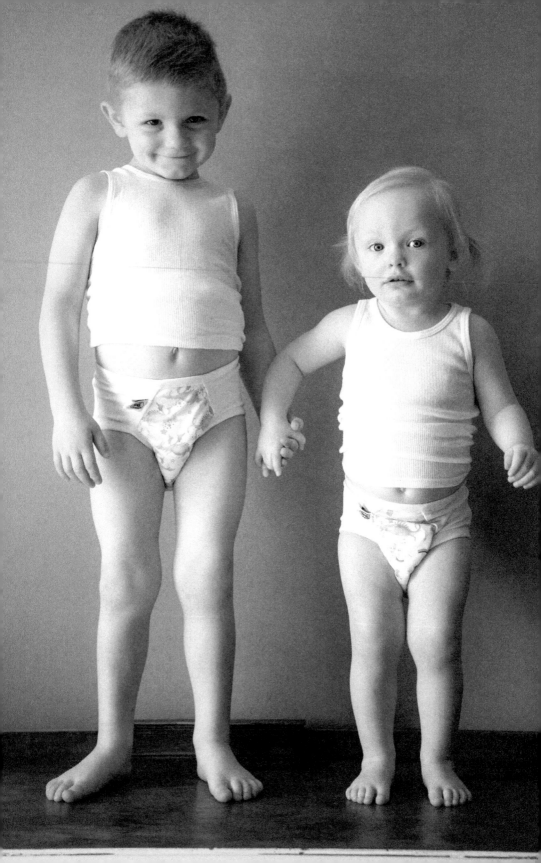

Potty Training Pants

Training pants are designed to be a transitional item to help children adapt between having an absorbent diaper to no protection at all in underwear. They are lightly padded, which helps catch leaks, but will also leave a child feeling very wet and having to "deal" with the accident. They can be essential teaching tools in the transition between diapers and being potty trained.

<u>Do I need training pants?</u>

No. Well, maybe. A parent who is savvy and ready for potty training—one who is confident, consistent, who knows what they're doing, and is determined to get the job done quickly—may not need training pants at all. They will go commando and stay on it, no matter how long it takes. They will clear their schedules, stay home for a few days or more, and be ready to tackle any accident when out and about. They will be prepared. Their attitude will tell their child that they mean business and they will have tactics in place to counter any usurping of authority. And they will potty train.

However, there is a whole other side of parenting that does take transitions seriously and believes that children need time to adjust to this new, permanent way of life. Neither school of thought is wrong. You need to determine what will work best for your family.

One thing is for certain, though: ***Disposable pull-ups are not training pants.***

We will get back to more education on training pants and how to use them in a moment, but we do need to be very clear here. Disposable pull-ups can actually hinder your potty training process because they are so good at absorbing! In fact, a pull-up is nothing more than a diaper without the adhesive side tabs. If we wanted to teach our children how to pull their pants up and down, we could just let them dress and undress themselves. Wait ... you probably are already. Problem solved, then! There is no need for pull-ups!

See, a child has a psychological bond to their diaper. They've been in it as long as they can remember. Since day one, it was there. As long as you have been there for them, so has their diaper. Giving them a virtually identical item to replace something and expecting them to learn an entirely different way of living because they now have a pull-up on (i.e., a diaper in disguise) is just not going to work.

Pull-ups are crutches for the parent. And if you find that you would feel much better about potty training if only you could use pull-ups, then please consider the new, modern-day cloth training pants options that follow. I assure you that they are much more effective in potty training than pull-ups.

Cloth Trainers

In order for training pants to be an effective transitional tool, they must meet the following criteria:

- Trim fitting.
- Mildly absorbent.
- Underwear-like in appearance.
- Causes the child to feel wet when used.

Examining the criteria above, you can see two things: why disposables do not fit the bill in any form and that trainers must truly bridge that gap between diaper and underwear. Each criteria sits somewhere between a diaper and underwear—absorbent, but kind of, not fully like a diaper. The slight padding of training pants is very helpful to sensitive children because they mimic the same feeling that their diaper already has. Typically, the padding in a cloth trainer is the same thickness as an unused disposable, so the garment feels good to the child. The kicker comes later when he pees and feels it!

Cloth trainers can help with poop anxiety.

Many children in this current generation seem to be having much more poop anxiety than in previous years. Perhaps this comes from our own fast-paced, tech-driven lives. But, one thing I can say is this: Think about how often a child has pooped in his life. Yeah, like every day a few times a day. It's always done in some standing or squatting position. It may even be done in a certain place. Some kids hide behind a couch or in a closet! But no matter what these variables are, the same consistent factor remains, which is that poop fills the diaper and is squashed into their skin (eww, I know, but just hang in there).

Taking a kid from years of this behavior and saying, "Now sit on this big toilet and let it all just fall away. Oh, and it will be cold and drafty instead of warm and soft, and your feet will be dangling, and you'll be in the bathroom instead of your closet,"—or at least they won't have the option to choose where they are—just might lead to a backlash in a willingness to comply. Yup. Not a battle I want to knowingly go into. My point is, just think about how sensitive your child is to change. Some don't really care and some fight change tooth and nail and need slower transitions.

Some parents tell me their children are potty training just fine, but when they put a trainer on them, the kid just pees or poops in them and doesn't seem to care. Well, why should he? This was how it always was before. He never had to care about pooping in this diaper. Only you cared. He is just slipping back into old habits. But, you will certainly be much better off using trainers instead of underwear, if you have a child with this mentality. Whether it is training pants or underwear, your kid may not care either way if he wets or poops. Trainers contain things better. Much better. Thin, mildly absorbent, and waterproof trainers will contain stuff even better and make your life easier. Waterproof trainers also hold wetness on the child's side, upping the wet feeling they will get when they pee.

How many trainers will I need?

You want to consider your laundry ability and your level of activity outside the house when answering this question. For a child, often at home and potty training, you will eventually level out at around six pairs. In the beginning, you will have a few accidents that will cause you to go through them more quickly, which is fine. But, letting some accidents happen outside the trainer is also a benefit. During your first two to three days or so, you may find yourself wishing you had ten pairs, but usually you can get by with a few and have one left over for the emergency car bag.

If you are out and about often and/or you find your laundering capacity to be more limited than a load a day, you will want to have more trainers on hand. The same goes for day care situations. Many day cares like to be provided with the same trainers parents are using at home, which will look like two sets of six to ten. In any situation, ten pairs of training pants are going to be enough to get you through twenty-four to forty-eight hours and possibly have one on hold in the diaper bag.

<u>What is the difference between them?</u>

Training pants vary widely in price and features. Through much trial and error, I've found some surprising information that can certainly be related to cost.

Here's What Happened When I Bought Gerber Training Pants

I'd like to share with you my very first experience with cloth trainers. As you may or may not know, I can sew. It's a fun, dying art that leads to relatively instant gratification on a job well done. So, when we went into potty training with my first child, I went out and bought Gerber training pants because I thought that's what you do. It was a three-pack for eight dollars, I believe. You know the kind. You've probably seen them in big-box stores. They looked like they were made of cotton, they kind of looked like underwear, and they had high side tabs that wrapped around the waist.

Now they have fun colors, but back then all they had was white. But as I said previously, I can sew and I had fabric! I was going to pimp out these trainers and make my boy fall in love with them. Then, he and Gerber would start this complex relationship for the next few weeks that would eventually lead to him getting potty trained all on his own. All I had to do was make him love these things.

I cut my fabric and began what should have been a simple process of folding under the raw edge and sewing straight stitches down the sides and along the top and bottom of the undies, but dang it! My needle broke. No big deal. I'll just replace it and move on. Then again. My needle broke within the first five stitches! And that's when I got suspicious. "What voodoo did this?" I thought. How can a mere children's apparel item take down my whole home sewing operation? And going out to Jo-Ann's to get another pack of needles was turning into a trip I didn't feel I owed to Gerber.

So, I took my thirteen-inch Fiskars and cut those training pants in two, seeking the mystical powers it held. Well, I can only sort of describe what was inside. It was a plastic mesh sponge that looked like a fabric at first glance, but it certainly did not feel like it. Not a textile, mind you. A very strange critter indeed. Like a loofa in your shower! Not the poufy one on a rope, but the scratchy one no one really uses, even though they bought it because it looked all nature-loving. A nice, thin slice of that stuff inside those bad boys. Only this loofa slice was made of plastic or acrylic.

Wow! I was just amazed at the lengths some big-box companies would go to in order to not spend money on what should have been in there and trick the public into buying something that wasn't what it seemed. I had been duped. I went on to try and use my other two pairs that I hadn't mutilated, but I was pretty disappointed on a few levels:

Level one

The side tabs that seemed overly large and substantial actually weren't. Although they were tall, they were only one layer of fabric thick and the cotton was a cotton jersey, like your T-shirt. This means there was no "hold" to the fabric and within minutes of wear, it loosened up and started getting super baggy on my little guy. Also, they started falling down. Even the binding that was around the legs was deceptive! It was just binding, no elastic. It completely lost its shape as it sagged on my boy, adding to my disappointment.

Level two

In Southern California, you don't always need to wear pants. Heck, I think even adults can get away with not always wearing pants "because we have a bathing suit on." So, there we are on a beautiful day, getting ready to head to the store. Like a good mommy, I made sure to not dress my potty training toddler in pants, so that I could attend to any accident quickly. I buckled the boy in the car seat and as I was doing so, that charming little man peed on me. Well, he had his Gerber trainers on, so I guess he peed on them. But what I saw was a little interesting. The compression of the seat belt in the padded area as he peed caused the pee to come straight out of the undies like they weren't even there. It was then that I understood the inner fibers were nothing more than space filler. Like rice in your dog's food. No nutrition. I mean, no absorbent value at all.

Training pants are supposed to be able to buy you a few seconds to get your child to the toilet in the event of an accident. With no fiber that actually locks in moisture, I think that these Gerber training pants are counterfeits.

There are so many great options out there now, though! You pay a little more for them, but they do their job, they are easier to use, and you feel better in this tough process. You truly do get what you pay for, in this instance.

What to Consider When Researching Trainers

How many pieces are sewn together to construct the trainer?

If the training pants you are considering are a one-piece front to back with binding at the legs and waist, they may be more poufy on your kid. Take one further step of research and search for those particular trainers on Google.com, then click the "images" tab and see all the home-based pictures there are of children in those trainers. This will give you a good idea of how they will look and fit on your kid and also how they might fit under clothing. Training pants made with more patterned pieces could cost a little more because of the additional labor, but those extra pieces will craft a better fit.

PUL in the wet zone

PUL is an acronym for polyurethane laminate and though it is a cloth that sounds like some scary stuff, it's actually not. A disposable diaper is made out of plastic and so it is waterproof. Likewise, PUL can provide waterproofing to cloth. It is when you take a thin layer of polyester and then place on it a one-millimeter layer of laminate. A heat transfer process then binds those two layers together, making them one, and you have PUL. It is very different—much thinner and more pliable—than the fabric from a shower curtain, which is made of vinyl. PUL is very thin and amazing at what it does. It is possibly one of the biggest reasons the cloth diaper industry has been so forward-moving in the past decade.

Some training pants rely on padding in the "wet zone" and some trainers take it a step further and line the wet zone with PUL. As self-explanatory as the wet zone may be, I will clarify it anyway. The wet zone runs from about three inches below the belly button down through the legs and up to the butt area. Training pants can include this waterproofing in this place only or take it farther from the very top of the belly to the top of the butt. Some trainers put their PUL inside, sandwiched between layers of cloth so you can't see it. The trainers featured in this book will be fully explained as to if they contain PUL and how much of it.

Leg construction: fold over elastic (FOE) or casing

Fold over elastic is just what it sounds like. In trainers, it is typically seven-eighths of an inch and folded in half to hold the fronts and backs of the edges, while providing stretch and give at the same time. It results in a smooth finish.

Casing can be done in two ways. An included casing is when a piece of elastic is applied internally to the edge (leg or waist), then folded inside out, revealing a finished, professional look. Then, there is a top stitch placed a half inch from the edge, which creates a casing, or tunnel, that the elastic is held in. An included casing could be constructed over PUL in the wet zone, making a trainer less likely to leak through those areas. It results in a bunchier, stretchy edge and will be a bit thicker than FOE.

An external casing is when a wider piece of fabric is folded in half and a thin piece of elastic is added inside that fold. That casing is then added to the legs and waist of the trainer. This gives a nice, smooth look and feel to the trainer. This type of casing is usually not waterproof. Both of them are still good and respectable choices. The trainers we feature in this book will tell you what type of leg and waist elastic they use.

Pocket for additional absorbency

It is getting more popular in modern trainers to have an additional thin piece of fabric sewn inside for the sole purpose of holding another piece of absorbency in place. You cannot tell from the outside of the trainer if it has a pocket and you certainly don't need a pocket for it to be a good trainer.

Since training pants are supposed to be lightly absorbent, adding a cloth pad into your trainer could work against you. Providing too much absorbency will take any natural consequence off the child if he has an accident and it is in those moments of natural consequence that we teach potty training.

There are, however, appropriate times for using more absorbency. When potty training naked or using cloth trainers, going back into a diaper when you need to leave the house can really set the process back. You are now teaching your child that he only has to do this when it is convenient for you and him. This can open up the door for a mindset that says potty training is just one option among many. Children craftily revolt later by purposely peeing their pants over and over again and if parents aren't prepared for this, they find themselves thinking they have potty trained too early and go back to diapers.

Well, we could just use an insert and make the training pants more of what we need them to be, without changing the look and feel of it, right? Right! You can also use an insert when you put your toddler down for a nap. I tell parents this...

"When you think to yourself, 'I WISH I wasn't potty training right now,' it's time to use an insert."

Potty Training Know-How

This is the most simplistic statement of how to potty train - Redirect the action. That's all any training is. You will be redirecting the action of eliminating to the proper location. Over and over and over again. There are plenty more things to say about how to potty train. I just want you to memorize this simplistic formula.

I'd like you to think of potty training as a group effort. I'm writing this how-to from the perspective of teamwork, wrapped in some fun. The elements here are introduced like a game. You can follow this fun, game-themed way of potty training, called The Elimination Game, or just take the instructions from it and run with them.

Two Weeks Before

Create Your Team - Members of your team will include the potty training toddler plus the adult support around them. There will be team activities, beginning with The Game Plan below. Start by getting your toddler on board and deciding who else is part of the team!

> *"We're going to do something big here and I want you on my team for this. We're going to play The Elimination Game! It's going to change our home forever and you're going to become a really big kid! Let's plan it out together!"*

Start your planning - Sit down with your team and go over a few things.

- <u>Set the day the game starts</u>. Use a calendar and plan for at least two weeks in the future.
- <u>Name your team</u>. This is optional of course, but you will have some team activities in the future and it may be fun to have a name.
- <u>Discuss who is on the team</u>. The team will shop together and do some activities together. If only one parent will be part of this, don't make both parents part of the team. The parental bystander can be the Cheerleader!

- <u>What will we need to get?</u> Make a list together of the stuff that will be helpful. Check out the Potty Training Products section to make the best informed decision for your team. Let your toddler help! We've included full color pictures so they can get a good handle on the products.
- <u>How the game will be played</u>. This is a brief overview. On our game day, we will stop using diapers and see how many times we can catch our pee and poop in the toilet.
- <u>Begin using the Potty Tracker</u>. This is not a team activity. The Potty Tracker is explained at the end of this chapter.

Start your shopping

Take your toddler with you and make sure he knows this is a Team Activity. Choose your items based on functionality. Feel free to shop online, as well. Kids like doing things that adults do and we shop on the computer all the time!

Prep skills to work on this week

- <u>Hand washing</u> - Do this before and after every meal. Start having your toddler wash his hands after diaper changes. You may want to check out the faucet extender in the Potty Training Products section to make hand washing easier and grow your child's independence!
- <u>Pants up and down</u> - But mostly down! You can always sing the Head, Shoulders, Knees, and Toes song to familiarize movements!

- <u>Getting dressed</u> - Aside from accidents, your child may need more outfit changes. Letting them do this themselves gives them a sense of accomplishment and pride. It will help build their self-esteem and empower them to do bigger things!
- <u>Visit other facilities</u> - When you start potty training (The Elimination Game), you will be home for a few days straight. Then, take just small trips out. While your toddler is still in diapers, start visiting other bathrooms as a Team. If you are at a restaurant, sneak away and check it out! If it's cozy like a home bathroom, mention that. If you're in a department store, go check it out! Don't freak your toddler out by surprising him with a commercial industrial child sucking, flusher monster when he tells you he needs to go later on. Remember, this will help with a smoother transition!

Prep your toddler for "teamwork"

Start playing age-appropriate games together. There are classics out there that are very inexpensive to buy, like Candy Land and Hi Ho! Cherry-O. Play games together often. It is helpful for you to be on a team together against someone else! You move the piece and your child spins the wheel. Bring your child into laundry time with you. Turn it into TEAM LAUNDRY and have your toddler pull out all the socks! Your goal is to actively and intentionally teach your child the abstract notion of people working together to the same end. Teamwork. This will come into play when you start the Elimination Game!

Two weeks before potty training, check over this list and make sure you are hitting these items:

_____ Go over the calendar to see how many days are left before we quit diapers and start the game.

_____ Mention there will be no more diapers.

_____ Talk about where poop goes. You can have your toddler show you. If he only shows you the small potty, take him to the big potty too and tell him it will go in the little one first, then the big one.

_____ Begin to visit bathrooms when you are out and about.

_____ Have kid wash hands after diaper changes.

_____ Your family is on board and has been notified of your start date.

_____ Your toddler has joined The Team.

_____ You have had your toddler practicing wiping (with cloth sitting on a chair or the couch. Watch form and help him correct things).

_____ You are counting down on a calendar each day until the potty will be usable.

_____ You are having conversations about the topics listed in How to Talk and What to Say.

_____ Clear your calendar or block off the next three to four weeks as you engage in the GAME.

This is a tip just for you and your partner. You've got two weeks (or more depending on when you start) to figure out what your child's cues are. No doubt, something about your child changes when they are "going" in their diaper. Typically, a child stops for a moment. If they are urinating, they might stare. Their eyes don't necessarily shift off their toy or from what they were looking at, but they just stare through it for a moment. There could be grunting when they poop or a bit of a squint. Watch your child now for these cues. If you can get down solidly now, you will be able to catch your child in the act quicker when it's time to play The Elimination Game.

The Potty Tracker

Wouldn't you like to know when your child is about to go? Wouldn't it be great if you knew they would be about every fifty minutes?

This is a chart available as a free download on SuperUndies.com. The idea is this. Every thirty minutes, you will check your child's diaper. You will not engage in any potty training. Just simply check you child's diaper. Mark on the potty tracker if the diaper is wet or dry. Put a W for wet, and a D for dry. You should also mark when your child has a bowel movement (mark BM or POOP) and when they are sleeping. Do this for seven days, although you may have collected enough data in four days to get an accurate picture.

Once you've collected your data, calculate how many hours your child was awake on day one and translate it into minutes. If your child was awake for eleven hours, then you would multiply eleven hours times sixty minutes. They were awake for 660 minutes. Now, count how many Ws you have on day one. If you had twelve "wets" and divided it by 660 minutes, your child peed on average every fifty-five minutes. Do this for each day.

Now, take your average minutes per day, add them up, and divide them by the number of days in your data set.

Day 1 - 55 minutes
Day 2 - 49 minutes

Day 3 - 52 minutes

Day 4 - 48 minutes

55+49+52+48 = 204 minutes.

Divide 204 minutes by four days and you get fifty-one-minute intervals.

NOW YOU KNOW! Your child can hold urine, but eventually pees on average every fifty-one minutes. When you are setting a timer to keep going back to the toilet, set it five minutes before your known interval. This data will be golden for your potty training efforts!

Don't worry if your intervals don't look like my sample. Depending on the age of your potty trainer, it will look very different. Intervals might range from twenty-five minutes to 2.5 hours!

Start Time	Time Blocks	W - Wet
7:00 AM	30m	D - Dry
		BM - Bowel Movement
		Nap

Potty Tracker

TIME	DAY 1	DAY 2	DAY 3	DAY 4	DAY 5	DAY 6	DAY 7
7:00 AM							
7:30 AM							
8:00 AM							
8:30 AM							
9:00 AM							
9:30 AM							
10:00 AM							
10:30 AM							
11:00 AM							
11:30 AM							
12:00 PM							
12:30 PM							
1:00 PM							
1:30 PM							
2:00 PM							
2:30 PM							
3:00 PM							
3:30 PM							
4:00 PM							
4:30 PM							
5:00 PM							
5:30 PM							
6:00 PM							
6:30 PM							
7:00 PM							
7:30 PM							
8:00 PM							
8:30 PM							
9:00 PM							

Keep track of your child's diapering habits *before* potty training. Add up all wet diapers and divide by the number of hours in that day to get that day's Wet Diaper Interval. Then add up your 7 day intervals converted to minutes and divide by 7 to get your true Wet Diaper Interval. Use this data when potty training.

This method is recommended by **Laura Woj, The Scaredy Cat Potty Trainer**, and brought to you by **Super Undies**.

The Day Before

You've been covering a lot of info over the last two weeks and hopefully, your toddler is excited to start the Elimination Game tomorrow! You've put a lot of energy into making the transition as smooth as possible, educating your child on the world and how everyone else plays this same game! You need to evaluate things now. Do you feel like you know what you need to know to lead your child successfully through these next few days? Have you seen the capabilities of learning, understanding, and willingness toward you and your parenting in your child? Now is the time to change the date further if either of you are not ready. Don't start this game and not finish it and remember, you can meet up with me online for support. Laura Woj is a page, not a person. Find me there. Facebook automatically searches for "people" first, so Laura Woj will not be visible until you search for a "page." We'll get you into the Scaredy Cat Potty Training Facebook group and you'll be good!

If you proceed, here is your checklist of things to go over with The Team:

_____ What area will you operate in?

_____ Put a towel down on the floor and the potty on the towel.

_____ Get your toilet paper ready.

_____ Prep some cleaning supplies - plenty of towels and a spray bottle.

_____ Explain the Elimination Game (details to follow in that chapter).

_____ Get your low-grade incentives prepped, but out of reach from toddler hands.

_____ Put your cheerleading squad on notice.

_____ Remind your toddler when you go to bed that tomorrow morning, we won't be putting a diaper on.

The Elimination Game
(Or How To Potty Train)

The Team - You and your toddler and any other person actively participating in the training process.

Cheerleaders - People in your life that support you and will be on the sidelines, but not actively participating. Make sure they know their roles! They are not to "undo" anything you are doing.

Rules -

- NO ASKING. You will direct a child to sit on the potty, using your known intervals.
- Use your known intervals while watching for accidents.
- Catch every accident.
- Implement The Swoop.
- Follow up on accidents with a discussion.

How to score - A child who catches any amount of waste in the toilet or potty gets a prize! Check out the next chapter - Incentives.

Objective - The game is over when the child can recognize the need to eliminate and get to the toilet by themselves.

Expectations - This game takes two to three days of full-time play, with continual intermittent sessions until the game is over. Please plan appropriately.

I'm going to level with you here. There's a lot of material out there talking about potty training in three days, potty training in a weekend, and potty training in twenty-four hours. I could say that perhaps all that is very doable if you are an expert and have nothing else but potty training this child as your job. We don't, though. We are not getting paid an hourly wage to come out of our own lives and do nothing else. We have not been trained in this way. It is not our sole job with hundreds of potty trained children under our belts. Although we are putting forth the effort and reading a book, we are not going to set ourselves up for failure by expecting any such thing. These things take time. You may have a magical unicorn baby that can figure this out on their own, but that's unlikely. If you've already tried to potty train and your child is hard-set against a portion of it, it will take longer to move past that hurdle. If you've never done this before and follow every step of this book, prepping and teaching every step of the way, it could still take weeks. Remember, potty training is nothing more than redirecting undesirable behavior toward a new desirable behavior. This is called "shaping." You are now going to launch into a campaign to reshape a child's known way of being, but you've done your homework and brought them on board. So here's how it all goes down. You've got three levels in The Elimination Game.

Level 1 - Naked
Level 2 - Clothing
Level 3 - Independence

Let's extrapolate on the rules a bit more. This could also be called HOW TO POTTY TRAIN.

NO ASKING - Because you have the data that backs up how long your child can hold their waste, you will be able to direct them to the toilet better than they could themselves.

<u>Use your known intervals while watching for accidents -</u> Set your timer to go off five minutes before your known interval, then direct them to sit on the potty. You can use the big potty with a step stool and seat reducer (The Uppy 2 and WeePod Trainer are great items in the product section) or use the smaller potty. Every Swoop should be directly to the smaller, closer potty. But if you are using your intervals, you can choose which to use. It may be beneficial to use the smaller potty when your interval timer is up because your child will sit there for as long as it takes from this point. The small potty can be put in front of the TV or at least in a more interesting place than the bathroom. Remember - you KNOW they have stuff in them! You tracked it for a week and found wet diapers every X amount of minutes. Once you direct them to sit, wait. It could be five minutes or ten minutes. If your child is getting restless, they can get up and walk around a bit, but you need to watch them like a hawk. Only let them up for a bit, then redirect them to sit.

<u>Catch every accident</u> - You may catch success in the potty or you may catch success in the form of an accident after you let them up. That's where the Swoop comes in. After any accident, reset your interval timer. There is a lot of potty training advice out there telling you to take your child every twenty or thirty minutes, but if you did the Potty Tracker, then you KNOW what your child's natural rhythm is. You could be in for a lot less work than every twenty minutes if your child is on a forty-minute known interval. By using the known interval as a guide, you will be prepping their bodies to recognize the urge. If you are constantly emptying their bladder before it is full, they are missing out on the urge completely.

Please, please, please. Do yourself a favor and stay off your phone. Social media can take us away from reality so effectively that you can and will miss accidents. This takes diligence, but will pay off with faster potty training.

The Swoop - When your toddler starts to release something, this is when you act. You don't JUMP UP and GRAB THEM! That will startle them like crazy and maybe cause their urethra to clamp up! Just swoop in and glide their little selves to the mini potty and sit them on it. Be silent at first, be smooth, and stay calm. No jumping, no shouting, just a smooth swoop to the potty.

Plan on waiting a few minutes for their body to calm back down from the Swoop. Tell them to relax and try to push it (whatever it was) out again, now that they are on a toilet. If you're prepared to swoop in and have gone over this process in your mind a few times, you will be more likely to stay smooth and calm with it.

Watch for secretive behavior. Some kids would prefer to hide when they have to poop. Maybe they want to concentrate, maybe they feel exposed sitting in the middle of a room. If this is your child, offer to them to hide that potty. You can put it in a corner and clamp up a sheet to give them their own little potty fort. This will help keep drafts off their bum and will probably seem special enough and intriguing enough for a "hider" to use! Clamps are only $1 at Home Depot and an old sheet is free!

Follow Up With a Discussion - The Calm After The Storm- This is your teaching moment. In potty training and in life. The Storm refers to the big action that just took place. The Calm is when it's all over and things have returned to normal.

In potty training, this is after the Swoop, after sitting on the toilet and relaxing to try agin, after going back to clean up any accident - when things return to normal. It's now time for your discussion. The Calm after the Storm is when a toddler's brain is most primed to learn and adapt to a new way. They are in a perfect place to reflect on what just went down. This is where you get eye to eye with them and talk about what just happened. Keep it light and encouraging. You are pretty much going to give them a play-by-play of events and what will change as he gets better at the game. Draw them into it too if your child is verbal. When we participate in a discussion, it locks in our brains better. This becomes our Team Meeting.

Dylan, you just peed on the floor because you weren't wearing a diaper. Do you know you peed? Can you show me where you peed at? That's right! Could you feel that tingle in your tummy telling you that you were about to pee? (It's okay, if not. You are drawing awareness to the fact that a there is a tingle and he can pay attention to it next time.) So next time you think you might need to go, like when you had a diaper on, try to get to the potty and sit there instead, The potty can catch it, like that diaper used to! I'll help whenever I can!

The above is all there is to potty learning. Training is the practice of what we've learned. Let's check out these three levels you'll be facing.

Level 1- Bottomless

This is the morning of day one. If it's cold in your house, I guess you could crank up the heat. Honestly though, that might make you miserable. Nobody wants a miserable potty trainer and a miserable mommy stuck in the same room. Check out Imagine's Baby Leggings in the Product Section for a brilliant solution to this problem!

We can potty train bottomless here and there, but you CANNOT stay here for long. You can be touch and go with the bottomless method, but parents who potty train toddlers bottomless for days at a time are actually reshaping the behavior to something that is not a complete thought. The child commonly begins to understand the notion of not letting his waste fall anywhere on the floor, so he redirects it successfully to the potty. But, when clothing comes back on, they instantly eliminate in it, whether it's pants, trainers, underwear, or a diaper (which it shouldn't be). After all, this is still a valid way of dealing with waste, is it not? To them it is, my friend. Go bottomless in the morning to help your child SEE what's happening. They need to learn where this stuff is really coming from. We've prepped them for what an accident will feel like. If you need a few bottomless sessions, fine. But, switch it up with clothing or trainers. You can stay naked on day one or half of day one. Any longer than a day and you're in danger of shaping the wrong behavior.

Level 2 - Clothing

Here's the truth. You can't stay naked when you're potty training. The rules of The Elimination Game above are all you need to be successful in catching and teaching these new toilet practices, but being naked is just one tool we use for teaching. It is not our only tool. When clothing comes into play, your words become very valuable.

Move on to trainers, clothing, or commando immediately. Once your child begins to sit and stay on the potty and once you guys are rolling in The Elimination Game, you must casually put pants back on them. Start off with loose pants and no underwear. This is called commando. You can use shorts or skirts, as well. You might have an immediate accident once the child gets pants on them. This is because of that Pavlovian response we were talking about earlier: an external influence causing a biological response in us. A hugging garment around the private areas feels like a diaper. Diapers equalled immediate elimination, without even consideration. It's what they've always done. Before THEY even know it, they've peed. Whether it is a pair of pants, underwear, or a trainer, follow the formula above and focus on your follow-up discussions. Continue with intervals. Reset at every accident.

Discussions now must include the feeling of the clothing. Don't worry if your child is nonverbal. Start out your discussions by engaging them in the conversation. Ask them questions they can respond to with pointing. After they have been fully engaged, it's time to teach.

Darla, did you just go poop? Where were you when the poop came out? What do we use now to catch the poop? When you feel that pressure on your bottom, you need to start getting to the potty quickly, so it can catch it! Can you run there now to show me the way?

If you are using incentives, ask the child to show you what they get if the poop falls in the toilet instead of in their pants.

By using words like "the potty catches the pee" or "the poop falls in the toilet," you are setting them up for what could otherwise scare them. Children can develop anxiety about poop and the possibility of losing it. A diaper offers a smooth transition from body to trash, but saying "the poop falls" preps the child for reality. It gives them permission to accept this. I know, I know. It sounds crazy. Just trust me.

Trainers will be a major asset even when your child is already potty trained. Invest in some good ones, because they can really help ease the stress of having a newly potty trained child. Kids who know what to do, can recognize the urge, and help themselves to the toilet will still find themselves in situations where they can't hold it long enough. This doesn't mean you are not potty trained. This means your toddler has a small bladder! You can be in trainers for a year or more after being potty trained. Use them whenever you see an extended car trip coming up, a playdate, a shopping trip, or when heading to the park. Accidents happen and trainers make your life easier when they do, especially if they are waterproof. Trainers will feel the same as underwear, but they must also make the child feel wet.

Start planning small trips out

After a few days of training with your known intervals at home, start planning small trips out. Keep using your intervals so you know when the time may come for your child to use the bathroom! Remember all that prep we did? By now, your child has discovered other bathrooms and has already thought about using them. This will be a whole new exciting chapter for them and it may renew their interest in The Elimination Game.

Be prepared. Your child is going to need to pee right after you get up to speed in the car, even if you had him try to go before you left. It's just part of the game.

Your toddler will also surprise you with needing to use the facilities when you are on the opposite side of a large department store, even though you asked him when you first walked in. It's just part of the game.

Think about it this way. There are a lot of aspects to this game that you are controlling. Your toddler stopping the world to find the bathroom is now his way of controlling things. It's a give and take. Just patiently play the game.

You should not be starting up your mommy and me playdates yet. Just small trips out for now. If you head out for longer periods of time, you will have more accidents, which is fine, but you don't want so many that it seems like you are going backward. You want to keep success a strong theme here, so set yourself and your toddler up for that success.

Level 3 - Independence

Independence is the ultimate piece to potty training. When you feel that you have reasonable success in catching elimination and when you feel that your child has a good handle on what is going on, it is time to teach independence. This means we need to create a more intense urge sensation.

At this point, your intervals need to get longer. In order to develop a stronger urge sensation in your child, you should add on five to ten minutes to your intervals. This will allow more time to fill the bladder, which tingles when stretched. That, my friend, is the urge sensation we are looking for.

Recognizing the urge is the real meat behind potty training. The rest is just "getting there." Working on the urge through your entire potty training process will help solidify this quicker. Watch for signs of wiggling and be especially alert when your child is distracted. Those are the times your toddler will need you the most. The pee-pee dance or wiggling around gives you a perfect opportunity to teach. Ask your child if they feel like they need to go. Draw attention to the reason behind the wiggle. They are so imaginative at this age that they oftentimes don't feel their own bodies. It's your job to transfer this.

Believe it or not, children need permission to act without their parents. Toddlers have been under their parents' watchful eye from the very beginning and have had to ask for help all the time. Don't forget to empower your child to own this! Once they hit Level 3 and understand the urge, they need permission to act on their own! Invite your child to go use the potty whenever they need to. They can always come back and let you know. You would love to celebrate with them! This is a household invitation only. Make sure they understand that they always need you to be with them when you are out.

Side Note

This is a wonderful time to have the stranger danger conversation, but don't do it in the context of potty training. It is just a random conversation you will want to start repeating with your children once a month or so until they understand it. As they get older, you will still need to repeat it every so often. This conversation is not to strike fear in the hearts of our children though. Just talk about how getting separated from Mom when you're out is scary, because the world is a big place.

I always taught my children that if they ever get separated from me, find another mom with kids. It's better than telling them to go to the nearest adult. I think it's even better than telling them to find a person in uniform! A mother will instinctively keep that child safe and start looking around to lock eyes with a frantic parent.

When The Boy was four, we had our first and only experience with a missing child. He wandered off in Toys "R" Us. We had a special visit from Grandma, who flew in to see her grandchildren. It was her tradition to take the kids to the toy store and buy them something when she arrived. While we were at the store, The Boy was looking at something next to Grandma. I thought they were together, so I turned my attention to my other son. Well, Grandma has not been a mother for years. She didn't understand that when she has a child, she is in charge of that child until the baton is passed on. She wandered off and he was left alone. It was about five minutes later when I saw her again - without The Boy. We instantly panicked and started searching the store. I told them not to put it on lockdown, but watch the doors. He could be outside! We ran the aisles quickly and didn't find him. Peter ran out one door and I ran out the other. Within moments, my eyes locked with another mother who was looking up and scanning the crowd. She had my son.

Moms are the nurturers. They aren't scaryand they are familiar to young kids. They will be easiest for a young child to approach. My son found a stroller and approached the mom, who did just what I thought she would do. Hang tight, knowing someone was on the lookout. If you have a toddler and want to start teaching this concept, tell them to find another child. They will be less intimidated by children and that parent will see the missing child and ask where their parents are. It might not happen to you, but it might and I hope this helps.

The truth is, kids run off for all sorts of reasons. Using the bathroom could be one of them. Treating home potty training and out-of-the-house potty training differently is completely acceptable. In my home, children don't have to ask for water. I would purposely place healthy snacks on a lower shelf of a kitchen cart to encourage them to help themselves. There were apples, bananas, and rolls readily available. Water is an "anytime" drink. Sugary stuff is controlled. Apples are an "anytime" food. Cookies are controlled. The bathroom is an "anytime" thing. TV is controlled. Feel free to make the distinction in your home, with the rules that suit you best.

Diapers at Nap and Night?

Feel free! You can explain it like this. If they are asleep, their body may not feel the urge to go potty, so they could end up wetting the bed. This is the only reason we wear diapers. If you get into a situation where your child starts to hold everything in until they get their nighttime diaper, switch to cloth. In fact, switching to cloth could help your child train faster at night. Super Undies have two pull-on style options for children training at night or that wet the bed. You will find the Hero Undies in the Product Section of this book. The Hero Undies start at size 0, which fits two-year-olds, and they are the most waterproof cloth option on the market. If your child is holding everything in until they get their nap time diaper, put a towel or waterproofing under them and use lightweight trainers for nap time. The Super Undies Pull-on Undies 2.0 are thin underwear-like, waterproof trainers that fit this bill perfectly! Children who seem very attached to their diapers and will hold everything in until they get one have typically been in disposables their whole lives. Switching to cloth can help break the cycle. It just doesn't feel the same as a disposable. We will cover more on nighttime elimination in Bedwetting and Night Training.

Incentives

Sure, you can potty train with incentives, but there are some things you need to know first. Any incentive needs to be something your potty training toddler wants, so he will work to get it. However, incentives can create an entitled response in a child. You are now bartering for something. They get a gift or prize if they give, which to them means that you get something if you give. If either one of you decides to stop playing that game, it ends. Not good for potty training. But here is the other side of it.

Young children do well with minor incentive prompts. Children twenty months or younger will work for the reward and not reason it through any more than that. If you're potty training young, feel free to use incentives, but there will be an awkward gap on coming out of that place. Make sure you set expectations in the right place from the very beginning. Your rewards will not be a forever thing. I break incentives down into levels, so you set the bar appropriately the first time.

Low incentive items: An item that is abundant, common, and pleasurable to your toddler.

- A hug.
- Stickers.
- Apple slices.
- Clapping.
- A silly dance.
- A special funny face Mommy or Daddy makes up.
- A phone call to or from someone special.

These items can be renewed indefinitely without causing harm. They work best with potty trainers twenty months and younger, although plenty of toddlers over twenty-four months old can love these things too!

Medium incentive items: Something not given often, has a higher cost value, and/or appeals more than "just a little" to a child.

- Candy (because of the sugar addiction factor. Feel free to use your judgment here).
- Toys - a hot wheel car or Lego mini figure.
- Coloring book.
- Trip to the dollar store to pick one thing.
- Watching a TV show.
- iPad time.

This is typically candy. I am not opposed to using candy as a potty training reward. I think it fits in perfectly and keeps kids wanting more. It is typically necessary to use a higher reward like this for children twenty-four months and up. They reason more and are working to get more out of life. Be warned though, they develop the ability to manipulate around this time.

High incentive items: Rarely available, but highly sought after to the child.

- A small scoop of ice cream.
- A trip to the big toy store.
- An experience, like a local waterpark.
- Watching a TV show or movie.

It's more okay to flip flop on incentives when potty training a young child, but be very cautious of using incentives wrong when potty training children twenty-four months and up. Incentives need to be used well and be a strong motivational tool. Implementing a weak incentive, then having to raise the bar later, will send the wrong message. It teaches children to hold out for more and leads to a silent power struggle. There are two rules to follow when implementing incentives.

1. Any incentive must ONLY be given once it is earned. If you have offered an M&M for any success in the potty and give them one for sitting on the potty but not using it, then you are sending the wrong message. You just told your child that you make things up as you go along and maybe if they whine enough they can get what they want anyways. Be strong! The time will come when they earn it! Perhaps you could consider giving one or two M&Ms for peeing and five for pooping. Simply sitting and staying put for a few minutes is something that a child can do without an incentive. That becomes one of those "because I said so" times.

2. Your incentive must be thought through and specific. If your three-year-old loves the iPad and you decide to use it as his incentive, then after you begin potty training you discover that he is using someone's phone to play Flappy Bird (the game he loves most on the iPad), then you have been outdone. He gets what he loves most and doesn't use the toilet. Perhaps "electronic games" was the better incentive. OR, if you have a few sugar-laden treats offered throughout

your typical day, like cookies or cupcakes, then want to use candy as an incentive to potty train, chances are it will backfire. The child can get sugar another way. They don't need to work for candy when a cookie is right around the corner. Perhaps "your choice of something sweet" is the better incentive here.

In observing children, I have found that they love TV, electronic devices, and candy more than anything. In a young potty trainer, incentives are all around and simple things can easily please them. You may not need to touch those three big ones. In older children, find what they love and are willing to work for and use that. Take your time, think it through, and be sure that your idea will work. In a child who doesn't want to play the game and isn't incentivized easily, we start to work with Reverse Incentives.

Let me put this in a way that might shock you, purely so that you don't forget it. A Reverse Incentive is when you hold something hostage. Sounds mean? It's really just another term for "Earn your keep." With older kids, their environment can become their reward. Maybe we just don't turn on the TV until we pee. Or if you have a kid who will pee in the potty but won't go number two, maybe we don't turn on the TV until we poop? Please let me try to convince you that this is not mean. If your child knows what to do and is refusing to do it, why do you continue to give them every benefit and privilege that they refuse to earn? The household system now simply dictates that all members use the toilet.

Our children are so privileged. I'm okay with that, but not when our children won't comply with our wishes and our household guidelines. Older kids who know what you want from them and have proven in the past the ability to do this, need to work through their reasons for not participating. Asking them to earn something they really love can give them the kick in the pants, I mean motivation, that they need.

One woman I know had a three-and-a-half-year-old boy who would not use the toilet. He just never showed any interest. She waited for the "signs of readiness," but she never saw them. He had used it with success in the past, but then refused to continue. He saw the toilet as something to try, tried it out, and then moved on. She never led him to the point where she required this of him and now he was starting preschool in two months. She said they wouldn't let him start unless he was potty trained. She HAD to now, so she did. She used her environment as incentives and had her boy earn his privileges. Here is her short story:

There is a community water park that is very cheap. It is the highlight of their summer every year, and it opened in 2 two days. She told him he needed to be potty trained in order to go. It didn't seem to bother him - yet. Once it opened, she drove past it with him in the car, and of course he wanted to go. "Nope!" She she said. Not until you're potty trained. Let's go home and get that diaper off, then we will work on this. We can go to the water park when you learn to use the toilet instead of diapers. While they were potty training, she made it a point to drive by the water park on occasion and remind him what he is missing. He was potty trained in no time. She used a high incentive experience, but stuck to her guns until she felt like she could trust him. The water park experience that she held hostage was something she planned on doing anyway. It was their favorite thing to do all summer long. But it was a privilege, not a right, and he needed to now earn it.

There are things all around you that are wonderful privileges to your children. For older kids, just potty train because you expect them to and praise their every success. But if it starts to get hard and you've given it a good shot with plenty of time and you're still coming up against a lot of resistance, you have an ace up your sleeve. If you tell me that taking away something (for them to EARN it, remember) is not working, you just haven't hit on your child's leverage point. There's always something they value the most and it may not be TV.

This is not punishment. A punishment is a direct consequence for wrong behavior. This is life. If you don't go to work, you don't get paid. If you don't drive to the store, you don't get your groceries. If you only serve chicken nuggets, you might end up with a picky eater. If you don't go on date nights with your partner, you might grow apart. If you don't wash your clothes, you might start to smell badly because you never have anything clean. If you don't plant your veggies, you don't have a garden. If you don't use the toilet, you don't go to preschool. So if you don't use the toilet, you don't get to watch your TV show either.

This woman needed the catalyst of a preschool demanding a potty trained child to become convinced that she could do this. She let these other folks convince her of it. If you don't have that pressure, how will you convince yourself? This process is more about your leadership skills and the confidence you have in yourself than if your two- or three-year-old is ready. Once you become a leader, your children will follow.

"A Reverse Incentive is when you hold something hostage. Sounds mean? It's really just another term for earn your keep."

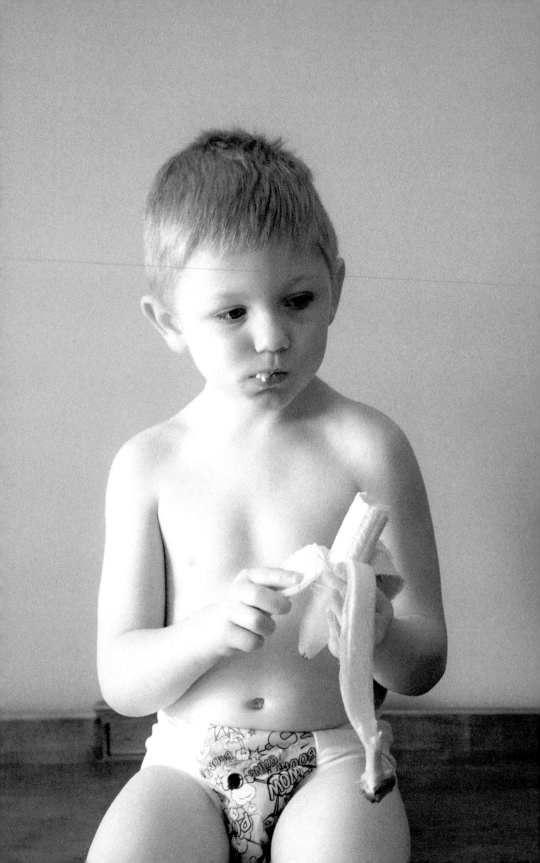

Regression or the Original ADD

It will most likely happen. To one extent or another, regression is common in potty training children twenty-four months and older. Kids are in the business of testing boundaries. It's natural and it's a part of growing up. Here's how it all plays out:

We started potty training and things were going great! We stayed home all day. We went bottomless. He really started to get it! We reinforced the skills on day two. We were flying. He went on the potty regularly and I trusted him in underwear. Then somewhere in week two, it all fell apart. He just started pooping in his pants and acting like he didn't even notice it. It didn't bother him at all! He would be playing at the train table, then standing in a puddle, without even looking up! What's happening here? Did my son forget everything???

OR

My daughter potty trained at twenty months old. It's been over a year since she's been using the bathroom and now all of a sudden she is having accidents every day. Sometimes, multiple times a day! Can she feel what's going on? Is there something medical happening that could be taking away her urge sensation? Did she forget everything? Did I potty train too young?

True regression can only happen if you had a potty trained toddler in the first place. If this was never the case, then you simply weren't done teaching the process and having them master it before you checked out. Go back to The Elimination Game chapter, see what level of potty training you two left off at, and then pick up the game from there.

There are a few reasons for a child to regress, so understanding them and figuring out which one it was will help you in your parenting. They either caught a temporary case of Potty Training Attention Deficit Disorder or they quit.

Attention

This is the beginning of your juvenile delinquent, trapped in a toddler's body, emerging. It doesn't matter what kind of attention he's getting. Attention is attention. This could be the very first diagnosis of (Potty Training) Attention Deficit Disorder. You child has a problem with a newly perceived deficit in the attention he's getting.

Was a new baby born? Did school start for an older sibling? Did school start for them? Did a parent's work shift change? Was there an accident or tragedy that happened? Did another sibling get braces and now gets more attention? Think, think, think. There is a reason your child doesn't feel that they are getting the same attention anymore and this is their sly little solution. To crap their pants. Yeah, it's pretty upsetting to us, but children don't have the knowledge of how germs and cleanliness affect people. They are young and there used to be all this attention over them in their potty training days. It was nice. Let's go back there.

On the other hand, a child who is in the middle of potty training is seeing life from a whole different angle! The attention that potty training brings them is simply magical! They get treats, they get the parents' full attention, Dad plays games with them, and Mom sits and reads with them. WOW! What a great world! Yes, they are absolutely, completely on board and excited with this whole notion of potty training. But once they master it, the attention fades. Now they are just supposed to do it. No one sits around doing nothing but watching their every move anymore. That was awesome and this is not. Let's go back there. And then there's the…

I quit

Did you know that kids love learning new things? Their brains are primed for it! If kids didn't have a desire to learn, they would never amount to what we all become. Kids are so good at learning that they could become completely fluent in two languages by the time they are five! So learning the process of using the potty and making that brain/body connection feels good and satisfying to them. Once they've mastered it, some of them are just done. They have more important matters to attend to, or rather, more fun matters at least. Maybe you think this kid might have forgotten what he just learned, but maybe he is smarter than you give him credit for. Think about it. What benefit is there in constantly having to stop what you're watching to go to the bathroom? Why should Batman have to stop saving Gotham City just so your son can go pee? Why should Mr. Fluffy Bottoms and Miss Petalsworth have to excuse your daughter from the tea party when she has to go potty? It was never like that before!

Some children just feel happy with the progress they made and want to go back to the way things were. Given your excitement over their newly found skills, they know you will not be happy about this change, so they simply don't include you in it. They just go back to peeing when they need to pee. Or worse. Maybe you can't yet agree that your child is that diabolical, but then again, you always did think they were pretty smart.

Think well, long, and hard about which category you think your regressive child fits into. Is he a quitter or an attention seeker? The solution is the same for either choice, but your parenting style for other things will change based on what you believe is the cause of this regression. If your daughter is just dastardly, then perhaps you'll be more on point for other things in her life. If your child is seeking attention, then perhaps you will carve out more time in your schedule to spend one-on-one time with her.

The solution

Don't go back into diapers, whatever you do. Well, unless you run into a really sick child who caught the flu and has diarrhea ten times a day. That's another story. But that's not what we're talking about. We are talking about a child who is regressing from potty training. Don't go back into diapers. Don't give in to what they want. If you feel bad for your child who doesn't think they're getting enough attention, then giving them back a diaper isn't helping anything. And if their schedule is just too busy that they cannot possibly fit in a bathroom break, then going back into diapers is also not the solution. This means you might have a lot more accidents on your hand, so brace yourself. Accidents just got a whole lot harder to clean up. Because they are going to clean it up. It would be easier if you did it, but they have to do it.

First of all, please understand that your little angel is still your little angel. She is not evil, even if she is conniving. It is our natural instinct to try and get what we want. Second, my solution to regression must be handled delicately. By delicately, I mean sweet as a peach with a cherry on top. You need to love your child thoroughly in this process – but you need to make him clean it up. All of us need to be held responsible on some level for our actions in order to grow. Your toddler is no different, regardless of their age, which is probably over twenty months old anyway. Typically, younger potty trainers do not regress in this fashion. They wait until they're thirty months to try and pull this card. If a toddler twenty months or younger is really having regression accidents, then perhaps they didn't understand the potty training concept in the first place. Perhaps they thought it was an option, instead of a necessity. This young potty trainer just needs to go back to square one and relearn the process, with the parents being intent on figuring out where the process is going wrong. We are talking about regression, true regression. A child who was potty trained and has now decided to quit.

In either situation, PT-ADD or the I Quit, your child will respond to cleaning it up themselves. Kids craving attention find it by cleaning up the accident. Kids who quit still love the attention! Mom is nice and sweet, I'm learning something new (again), and we are spending time together! That's the short of it, but it doesn't stop there. You have a trick up your sleeve. Here are the rules for the cleanup:

1. Parents are hands off. If the kid can do it, even though it takes forever or they struggle or they don't do a good job, let them do it themselves.

2. Parent explains every step of the cleanup process, then lets the child attempt it.
3. Parent micromanages steps. Break down every detail.
4. Parent makes this take FOREVER.

That's the key really, making it take forever. A child will love the attention at first and may even pee on the floor a few more times so you will do this with him, but eventually it won't be fun anymore. Eventually, it will take Sarah away from what she REALLY wants to be doing. You have to get past the fun learning part. You need to breathe deeply and persevere. Remember the chapter on The Fight? Your best assets were the element of surprise and you knowing the future. If you know that this will take forever, just clear your schedule and put things on hold. Call up your partner and have them pick up Taco Bell on the way home, cause you've got accidents happening and it won't be easy. I personally think Taco Bell is gross, but pick something easy for both of you. Yes it will cost you more, but this lesson is invaluable. Carry a glass of wine with you through the process, but don't eat Taco Bell while drinking wine. That's just wrong.

You may say, "Laura, how can the cleanup process take forever? It's not that hard."

Okay, let me walk you through what this could look like. Just think about every step from the capabilities of a toddler, so slow - things - down.

SOS - Mayday! Mayday!
THERE'S A PUDDLE ON THE FLOOR!

1. *Talk - be real. This is your matter of fact voice.* Honey, we don't go pee on the floor. You KNOW it goes in

the toilet. Remember when I taught you that? You did great. You can't be doing this anymore. You'll have to learn to clean it up in case this happens in the future. I'll tell you want to do.

2. Help him find a towel to throw on the wet spot before moving on. You'll come back to it a bit later.

3. Tell him to climb out of those clothes and head to the bathroom. *This is where sweet-as-a-peach takes over.*

4. Let's get cleaned up. Parent starts tub water. Climb in the tub. Here's the soap. *Child is now directed in the ancient ways of the splash bath. We are not taking a bath or playing with toys. We are just getting clean.*

5. Hop out of the bath now. *Parent helps the kid out of the tub. We don't want any slips!*

6. Let's go get new clothes. *Head to the bedroom to get new clothes. The child must choose his clothes and dress himself completely. If he needs help, just verbally walk him through how to do it. If he has to sit on the floor to pull his pants on, great. This could be the longest part of the whole process. If he can't get his shirt on, help him to take it off and let him try again. Let a few attempts go by, being sweet as a peach, before helping. Explain that this is important, because if he has another accident, he will need to know how to handle it. He has to know how to change his clothes if he is going to pee on them.*

7. Head back to the mess. Have him put the wet towel and his soiled clothing in the laundry or straight into the washing machine tub.

8. Have him wash his hands after touching soiled clothes.

9. Hand him a spray bottle to spray the floor.

10. Hand him a towel to wash the floor.
11. Have him put the cleaning towel with the soiled clothes.
12. Time to have him wash his hands again.

This will most likely take fifteen to twenty minutes, but now you have a mess that's all cleaned up and a sparkly, clean kid. If it happens again, budget another fifteen to twenty minutes. Remember, it will be fun at first, but eventually it will wear off. He will soon want to pee on the floor to show you that he can do all these new things by himself. Too much praise in this process will encourage him to repeat it order to gain more of your attention. Make sure you warn your child that after a few accidents, they will now have to do this on their own. They can call you to start the tub water and help them get out, but you won't be walking them through the process anymore. It will be their responsibility. If they don't want to participate anymore, then you now have a parenting issue on your hands, rather than a potty training issue. They simply don't move on in life. All of this is avoidable by using the toilet, so until it's done, no TV or game or toy or whatever. I understand you may not want to drag discipline into this, but remember, you are not disciplining over potty training. You are fine with them cleaning their mess up until they're twenty. You are just making them responsible for that job.

Here is the rainbow at the end of the tunnel. This process usually doesn't repeat itself more than ten times. You can verbally lead the first five cleanups, then hand them the reins. But make SURE you follow up! A job half-done then abandoned with no follow-up just taught your child they can get away with that. Not cool.

Bedwetting and Night Training

Let me be clear here. The majority of children are going to "nighttime train" themselves. There, that's it! Easy, huh? But that's not to say there are still some things you should know. I actually have a nighttime training method that you can try, but really, a child's body typically figures this out for itself. So what about the five million school-aged children in the U.S. who wet their bed? Yes, there is that. Chances that you will have a bedwetter are about 20 percent. One in five kids under the age of five will wet the bed. Four out of five won't, so the majority will night train themselves. This leads me to my next point. I had three bedwetters, which means that twelve other children didn't! The Boy wet until he was five, Boy number two wet until he was eight, and The Girl wet until she was six. Neither parent had bedwetting issues in their youth.

Potty training is a big shift and learning process for a kid's body. There is a lot going on in the body and a lot happening in the brain, but you have Mother Nature and instinct on your side. Naturally, our bodies are programmed to not eliminate in our sleep. Don't even worry about nighttime until you are completely solid on daytime. Once a child is consistently potty trained (that is, he can hold his urine and poop for a reasonable time and use the toilet on his own), then nighttime stuff can start to happen. If your child is potty trained, but having daytime accidents because they cannot hold it long enough to get to the toilet, his bladder needs some growing and stretching still. Bedwetting is just going to be a part of life until his body grows up a bit. The best you can do is keep everyone comfortable through the night. Diapers and cloth Nighttime Undies are a "go" at this point!

You will see a shift from dirty diapers in the morning now. You know you are well on your way to being potty trained when your child has no dirty diapers at night. It is one of the first biological shifts that takes place in this stage of life. A child who is having bowel movements at night is typically not potty trained and possibly needs more time to grow up. The body's natural progression is to stop pooping at night, but wetness can take longer to figure out.

It can take a child's body three to six months of being daytime potty trained to naturally figure out nighttime. You can consider yourself in the "night training" phase at this point. Just give it time. If after six months of mostly accident-free days your child is still peeing at night, "Hello bedwetting, nice to meet you." Let's lay out some help, starting with the easiest and least invasive to the most.

Night Training Method Number One - A Switch To Cloth

This method works the best with a child who has been in disposable diapers. Switch your child's nighttime disposable to a cloth option. That's it! By making this change, you are shifting what the mind is going through when the wetting actually happens. Kids can feel more wetness in cloth than in disposables, which is a huge advantage to a sleeping brain! It could even be powerful enough to help wake them up.

People have told me that after switching to cloth at night, their children just grew out of bedwetting in a few weeks. That is a relatively common occurrence and a few weeks is what it will take to re-program the brain/body connection. However, in the event this does not work, guess what? You have a cloth option that doesn't cost you money every time you go to the store! Parents spend an average of $400 a year on nighttime disposable diapers. They are more expensive than regular diapers and they know you're going to pay whatever their sticker price is. The price point per package is similar to diapers, but you get less and less quantity with each size you go up. With cloth, you can invest $60 in two pairs of high-quality, high-absorbency underwear that can last two to three years! Check out the Product Section to review some nighttime cloth options.

Night Training Method Number Two - Extra Sleep

There's nothing tough about this idea, except maybe the fight to get your kid to bed earlier! I list this as second in the order of ease and least invasive because it may or may not apply to toddlers. Kids in elementary school and toddlers with busy mornings don't have a choice in when they wake up. Naps start to go away and exhaustion sets in at night. There is a place in the brain that stays awake for the sole purpose of making sure you don't eliminate in your sleep. When your body isn't rested well enough, it is too deep in sleep to feel the signal of a full bladder. Nonetheless, the bladder must release. Getting thirty more minutes of sleep per night for a few weeks can be enough to restore your sleep tank and stop bedwetting.

Night Training Method Number Three - The Birthday Suit

Try having your child sleep bare-butted. When a child pees at night and the wetness is caught in the diaper, whether cloth or disposable, it is held close to the body. That limits the cause and effect feeling. If you want a real "wake up" effect, having nothing will give that to you! Sure, you have to diaper the bed instead. Sure, you have to wash a blanket in the morning. Sure, you need to budget time for a bath or shower the next day, but this is all temporary. Have your child sleep bottomless for three to four days straight, up to a week. Remember, you only have one opportunity each night (usually) for the learning moment to happen, so these methods are not a one-night solution. You will need repetition for the solution to take hold. After a few days, if you don't see any improvement, just go back to diapers or cloth overnight underwear. Try this method once a month.

Night Training Method Number Four - Night Waking

First of all, this method didn't work for us. Boy number two wet the bed until he was eight and this was the method suggested to us by his pediatrician. You are to wake up your child before you go to bed and have him walk to the bathroom, under his own power, then go pee. Well, we could never get to that "under his own power" part. He would swing at us in his sleep, yell at us in gibberish, and then try and turn over to go back to sleep! It was definitely worthy of videotaping and playing at his wedding, which I should totally do as payback for all the craziness he's put me through, but I digress. Night waking is supposed to be a conditioning response to a time until his body works it out. If you wake your son up every night at 11 p.m. and walk him to the toilet, he is supposed to start waking up on his own at 11 p.m. and have the urge to go pee, or at least this is how the doctor explained it to us. I've also read that you could begin waking your son up a littler later each night and move your toilet time deeper into the night, training his bladder to get fuller and pressing on those nerves harder. This gives children more opportunity to wake up themselves through the feeling, which is eventually where you need to get to. This is also assuming your child will wake up and walk under his own power. It takes weeks to months to get results. My doctor told us to do this for as long as it takes. She must have had a lot of faith in the method! If you have a kid who just can't wake up, then see Method Number Two. This is number four on the list because of its disruptive nature and length of time necessary to create any change.

Method Number Five - Alarms

A bedwetting alarm is something that feeds into your child's underwear. When a drop of liquid hits it, it either buzzes or makes a loud sound, startling your child awake. It is effective at creating the brain/body connection, by waking the child when he urinates. It is expensive, ranging from $100 to $200. Some people say their child can sleep right through it! This is number five on the list because of its high cost and the possibility it may not work.

Additional Notes on Bedwetting

Medications can affect bedwetting

Children on medication for ADD may have their sleep affected. The constant stimulation that these meds cause can make the child into a deep sleeper at night. It's best to leave these kids in a diaper or Nighttime Undies and let them sleep peacefully. Disturbing their sleep will make them more tired and cranky and they will be taking another dose of a stimulant in the morning.

On the contrary, there are medications that can help stop the production of urine at night, which will not stop bedwetting, but help until the child outgrows it.

Constipation can cause bedwetting.

I've heard stories of how training kids in the two- to two-and-a half-year-old range can scare them into holding their poop. This compacts it and causes a buildup. The enlarged bowel and colon press against the bladder, making it hold less and less. The constant pressure eventually affects the nerve sensation the bladder gives off and now you have frequent daytime urination and chronic bedwetting. The solution? Enemas. Yeah. Not happening in my home. The medical advice given stated that the majority of all bedwetting happens because of constipation, even minor constipation, and could be diagnosed with an MRI and alleviated with frequent enemas under a doctor's guidance. Is it worth it? Is it that big of a deal if your kid is wetting the bed? Regular enemas come with a whole different set of problems and we can start with the physiological effects of them. But I don't want to go there. I would encourage you to look into a more gentle solution, like stable diet alterations for a few months. Doctors want results right away and they will medicate or alter life to get them. My son was not constipated and pooped every day, sometimes multiple times a day. Yet, he wet the bed. It just wasn't a big deal. I just got him some Super Undies. No big deal. I found that he eventually became aware of his wetting and started to climb out of the Super Undies, leaving them on his bedroom floor and going back to sleep. His bed was dry and he was well-rested. I just threw the undies in with the next load of laundry. That was our routine until it stopped.

Talking to children about bedwetting

Parenting is all about leading, teaching, and guiding. We all have troubles in life. All of us! Not one of us gets away without dealing with things we have no control over. Such is life. Showing your child that you accept these things on his behalf and not making a big deal over them will aid you much in building your child's self-esteem. If you are always worried about it, seeing doctor after doctor, and sighing heavily when stripping the bed, then you are modeling behavior that will tear your child apart inside. Even having your child make his own bed if he pees in it can be damaging, depending on how you go about it. Make sure your child knows that this is not his fault and there is nothing you can do about it. In fact, it's not a big deal at all! It's just a part of life. I suspect our culture's diet may have something to do with it, but there's only so much we can change there, too. If you're not worried about it, he won't be worried about it. In my home (which is VERY playful) bedwetting jokes were off limits. Period. We modeled kindness and understanding. I also told my son that one out of every four boys in his class wets the bed. Statistically, boys wet more than girls. Ten percent of six-year-olds and under wet the bed. By seven, that number falls, but there is a discrepancy in boys versus girls. Twenty-five percent of boys in a second grade classroom are still wetting the bed. Giving these statistics to your child will help them understand they they are not alone! My son was so comfortable with his issue that he went to sleepovers with his Super Undies. We just told the parents and my son spoke to them, as well. It went like this...

"Uh, hi. Yeah so, I sometimes wet the bed, but I can't help it. I have these undies that don't make anything wet. If you still are okay with me sleeping over, great. It's okay if not though."

One hundred percent of the time, the parents were fine with it. And guess what? Most times we did this, his friend turned out to be a bedwetter too. Boy number two never wanted to wear a disposable overnight diaper. He saw them as "baby diapers" and preferred the company of cloth. It made him feel better.

Deciding Your Bedwetting Solution

If you find yourself with a bedwetting child, take that issue and apply it to your life. How much does it affect your day? Your night? Your child's self-esteem? If it's not a big deal, then don't go seeking out all sorts of ways to help. If your kid wants to see a doctor about it, tell him "Sure!" But let him know that it's not a big deal to you and that you will go see what the doctor says and decide what you do from there. I don't want you to go into a situation where you try and find a solution, then end up doing twice-a-week enemas or a regular dose of Murelax, which causes your child to poop their pants when they thought it was just gas and wonder how you got there. Let your child know that you will only entertain solutions that fit with your family. Or maybe you just wait for his next scheduled physical and bring it up then? There is less focus on that issue and the whole appointment isn't focusing on this "flaw." An appointment made for just bedwetting puts pressure on the doctor to provide you answers and a solution. Then, you have a follow-up appointment, of course. More focus on a problem that's just not a big deal. We're not in the business of breeding anxiety. We're in the business of parenting.

Potty Training Multiples

Let's cover two sets of multiples; - twins and siblings. It's delightful to hear moms come to me and tell me they want to potty train their two-year- old with their three-year- old!

<u>Twins</u>

Ask yourself this before deciding how to approach things. How close are your twins in similarities? Identical twins are the easiest to train, because their bodies are so similar. Boy/ girl twins can be very different, and should be assessed as to whether potty training at the same time is a good idea. I find that fraternal twins can be so different that they need their space and can use potty training as a form of stressing individuality, when potty training after twenty to twenty-four months. Twenty months or before and you can potty train any two children together without much fuss, whether identical or fraternal. This is because they are learning and being led, rather than reasoning things out for themselves. By twenty-four months, kids can reason. Twins can start to compete and get sensitive about attention. You really have to examine your twins to decide what stage they are in. If they treat each other well and get along great, than you are all on the same team! If they fight often, then consider them individually and decide who is ready and who is not.

If you decide that your twins are ready to potty train together, make sure you get two mini toilets. It will happen more often than you think that one child decides to sit down and the other immediately has to go, as well.

Siblings

Potty training siblings together can be a very successful way of going about it. You're capitalizing on peer pressure at its finest. It's a very common for the younger sibling to be more advanced and developmentally ahead of their older sibling at the same age, mainly because they have their developmental next steps modeled to them. Older siblings are often seen as heroes to younger siblings. They look up to them and want to do everything their brother or sister does. When potty training two kids of different ages, make sure you set the expectations for what you'd like to see out of them. Encouragement is going to play a big role here.

Here's how potty training two kids will work.

1. **Have two potties ready**. This is a great opportunity to get them involved and get on the team. They can pick out their own potties, so there is some individualized taste to the process. As you're picking out the toilet, go over how a toilet needs to function. Point out things like wipes or toilet paper that will need to be accessed and a cup that will be pottied in and have to be dumped into the toilet. Perhaps the ring cushioned seat can double as a toilet seat insert for the big potty. By going over the features you will need in the toilet, you are also helping to prep them for their jobs in using this toilet.

2. **Choose your incentives appropriately**. If one child is doing better than the other and you are handing out M&Ms, it will likely bother the other child. You don't want a kid to get so frustrated that he gives up. This can easily be the case if one child is peeing constantly in the potty, even going in small amounts in order to go more often, so he can get the reward. Meanwhile, the younger sibling is getting nothing. Use the Potty Tracker for both children to see if their intervals are similar. A great way to slow down incentives is to use Potty Training Punch Cards. This is a $5 item on SuperUndies.com. There will be professionally printed cards on stock, the same quality you would find in a store. They can also be printed out for free on your home printer. These cards will slow down the rate that a child will receive a reward. Every time you get success on the potty, you can have that child color in a circle. This gives you the opportunity to explain to both kids that once all circles are colored in, there will be a prize. You will have five conversations about this before one child gets the prize. and eleven conversations about this before the second prize is given!

3. **Don't use candy**. Candy can really frustrate a child when one is getting it and the other is not. Stay away from offering sweet things. Instead, offer small toys that they both can share if one earns it.

4. **Make the toddlers a team!** Tell your toddlers that they are on the same team, and team members root for each other. You want both kids engaged in this process, and both kids learning from the successes

and failures of each other. Most kids only get to learn first hand, but keeping the kids together through this gives them twice the opportunities to learn! When one kid starts to pee, get him to the toilet with the other kid in tow. Have the second child observe all that is happening with the first. Same with accidents. If one child goes on the toilet, you and the other child can clap and cheer for him! Don't let the more successful kid check out of the process just because he's got it already. Keep them involved in the cheering squad and have them stay together as a team. You can relax this a little after a few days, but not entirely.

5. **Enlist the help of others.** In order to play The Elimination Game successfully, you may need more than just yourself watching. Using your intervals will be very helpful, especially if they are similarly timed. But if you are having one child sit, the attention over using the toilet could cause the other child to have an accident. This is a difficult process with only one person. You are bound to miss something when your attention is divided, especially when you catch one in the act and swoop in. Your second child is bound to follow suit, either through Murphy's Law, a natural occurrence, or as an attention-seeking move.

6. **Work in shifts.** You need to be on point and watch like a hawk. Two parents and two grandparents are optimal for this. You can work as a team and take turns watching. I like the teams to shift around a bit, with the head Team Leader spending some time with each of the others. This may be the one who

is reading this book! The more in- tuned person into the method of potty training should coach and model how to parent through this, as well as show what to watch out for. Having the parents on different teams also helps reinforce the couple's parenting style to the grandparents. If Mom and Grandma work together, then Grandma is learning Mom's parenting style and how she handles accidents with her children. This will help Grandma be on the same page and copy this if and when she watches the children later.

7. **Day 2** - Work in longer shift. You could very easily be running out of steam now. It will be a big benefit to go out and feel normal. Switch team mates today if you'd like. Remember, parents and learning from each other too! Having three to four hours to do something for yourself will refresh you to come back and be on point again. Apply the steps covered in The Elimination Game chapter from this point on.

8. **Limit the main areas of your home for a longer period of time.** When potty training one child, limiting your areas may last for a few days, but when working with two children it will be easier in the long run to have a limited area for a two weeks.

Daycares and Nannies

Let's face it, you need them and they need you. We'll, I hope they need you. Things get easier when there is some give and take. A daycare that doesn't watch it's numbers and does not consider each account "valuable" will have a different approach with you in the event you don't agree on something.

There could be two different scenarios you find yourself in with daycares. They say it's time to potty train and you didn't see it coming, or you think it's time to potty train and they don't agree. If the daycare tells you it's time to potty train, congratulations! You now have an instant team working for you! Since daycares often have your children more than you do on the weekdays, they will be doing the majority of the work. Be sure to follow their instructions and ask any questions you have. Find out what you need to do to support their efforts on the weekend and make every attempt to aid them in this process. Daycares can have your child potty trained in a week or two if they have a good program in place. They typically have set criteria they use to determine when to start. For most daycares, they go by age. Twenty-four or thirty-six months is the magic number. We've talked about the issues that can occur in this age range, but with a solid, consistent team on your side training through the days, most of this can be quickly overcome.

If you think your child is ready, but your daycare doesn't agree, you still have a few options.

1. **Set an appointment with the daycare director.** Don't get frustrated with the staff just yet. Just casually talk about having potty training support and if the staff resists, thank them for their time, kindly. If you are frustrated with them, they will tip off the director, and she could be resistant to you, as well. A kind person approaching the head of the program can get further. Just set the appointment and state your case. If you are asked ahead of time what the meeting is about, tell them you have a concern with your toddler. That's it. When meeting with the director privately, you can discuss all the signs of readiness you see. You want to avoid saying things like, "I read that ..." or "I heard that ..." You want your opinions on the matter to be your own and whole heartedly believed by you.

2. **Potty train at home, regardless.** You can work systematically on the levels of The Elimination Game at a slower pace. Chances are your toddler is already telling you they have pee'd. Have some naked time, and when your child becomes more reliable with using the potty, transfer the responsibility onto your toddler to start telling you they have to pee. Invite them to not tell you and to just use the toilet as needed. Talk about the tingle, or tickle, that happens low in their tummy or behind their special parts. This is the final stage before you come out of diapers. You need to have this level of independence before you battle the daycare again. By now, your toddler is reasonably potty trained. Empower them to independently go to the bathroom at home whenever they need to, or to tell you they

need to go when you are out. This independence will transfer over to a daycare, babysitting, or nanny situation. It can also be used when sending your toddler to relative's house.

3. **Go along with the daycare.** Since they will be doing the potty training for you, waiting for them to get on board could be the easiest way to go. When a daycare has a potty training program, they are assuring parents they will be allocating resources to this specific task. They have many kids with a higher adult-to-child ratio than at home. Their decision to not potty train your toddler could be simply because they don't think she/he is ready, but it could also be because there are no other kids potty training. If they allocate resources to this task, they are taking those resources from the adult-to-child ratio. It makes sense for them to potty train multiple children at one time, and the children learn faster from one another in this way. If you see a potty training group already formed and in full swing and you really want your toddler in that group, ask if you can have her participate for a week and see how it goes. Tell them you really think she is ready, and if she doesn't perform well, you can stop. It's important to understand that the daycare attendants know their routines and capabilities. If they say it's not time, they could have a reason.

Nannies

This situation is completely different from daycares. Often times, nannies come and tell me their client's child is ready to potty train, but the parents are not on board. Without the support of the parents, a nanny will not receive the financial support necessary for the items needed to potty train. They won't receive follow-up support after hours, either. If you are a nanny and you are SURE you and the child are ready to potty train, and if you are in a position that puts you as the main caretaker, then approach your clients with that information. Also, complete the Potty Tracker and share the interval with the parents. Parents don't want come home from work and have to sit their child on a toilet every twenty minutes. If the interval is favorable, then they may be more on board. If you have a plan and can explain things clearly, as well as the parents' necessary involvement after your shift, then state your case.

If you are a parent who knows it is time to potty train, but are receiving pushback from your nanny, it's time to figure out why. Your nanny is not comfortable with potty training for either one of two reasons. She doesn't know how, or cannot find the time to fit this into the day. Pull back the playdate schedules and park times. Provide easier meals, if that is a time factor. Slow life down a bit. If your nanny is not educated in how to lead potty training, provide her with a copy of this book. Tell her to take on-the-clock time to read it. Have candid conversations about what the fear could be, or why she is resisting.

Potty Training with Special Needs

Special needs is a broad term. Many situations can cause delayed potty training, like Down syndrome or autism. Learning disorders or hearing issues causing speech delay can lengthen the time it takes to potty train, or when you begin, as well. My advice here can be applied to most situations, but you will have to determine the length of time necessary to stay on each topic. Read through this chapter for ideas, then work with your therapist to determine which approach you take.

Using a picture board is one of the best ways to transition to and prep for potty training. PECS, or Picture Exchange Communication System, is a series of cards that has a picture to identify a task, word, or object. I recommend using this system with cards specific towards elimination. Start with a learning phase where your child becomes familiar with the steps involved in using the toilet. Each picture is one step in the process. You can make your own, but there are cards out there that display the standard steps. Using cards that are separate can avoid overloading your child with information, which can lead to frustration. Start with small steps and work on the individual parts of potty training separately. Eventually, you will be able to build longer sequences with your cards.

The steps of elimination

1. Go to the toilet.
2. Pants down - (this can be practiced separately, then added in later).
3. Sit on toilet.
4. Wait.
5. Wipe.
6. Get up.
7. Pants Up.
8. Flush.
9. Wash.

You can group some of these things in your cards, simplify them, or break them down even further. Micro steps might include:

- Go to bathroom.
- Unbutton pants.
- Pants down.
- Sit on toilet.
- Wait.

And so on, breaking steps down as you see fit.

Do NOT include micro steps in something your child will innately do. Overcomplicating the system can cause an overwhelmed response. Watch your child for a bit and see what he or she understands already, and bundle that item with another step. If omitting it all together is possible because it is implied (like unbuttoning pants) and your child will know that, then omit it.

I've seen a great picture card of a child with an exclamation point hanging above his head, indicating the child feels the urge. PECS can be used with all children, whether special needs or typical. It can also be used for younger children who are not yet verbal.

Slowly teaching the steps of elimination will eventually be successful with the help of your team. Consistency is the key. Start slowly, take small steps, and stay consistent. The other elimination method that can be applied to a child with special needs is a routine-based elimination system.

Routine elimination

Routine elimination is nothing more than building a routine around elimination. If you can start to sit on the toilet every morning, do so! The younger the better, since you can truly just build in time on the toilet to your daily routine. The majority of families with special needs children start later though, so building in a routine will start slower. Just add one step to your day per week.

- Week 1 - Sit on the toilet when you wake up. Read a book.
- Week 2 - Sit on the toilet every morning. Read two books.
- Week 3 - Sit on the toilet every morning and read two books. Sit on the toilet after lunch. Read two books.
- Week 4 - Sit on the toilet every morning and read two books. Sit after lunch, and read two books. Sit after dinner. Read two books.

Perhaps week 1 doesn't start with sitting on the toilet though. You may need to build up to that. For a child who seems like they will be resistant, start by playing The Grounding Game. In psychology, there is a method of "grounding" oneself when you feel anxious. You are to touch five things around you and think of five things you are thankful for. This helps bring your mind back into reality, rather than the anxious place your thoughts were taking you. In the same way, a child who is anxious about change can become grounded to his surroundings.

The Grounding Game

Start in one room of the house, a place where your child is comfortable. Perhaps this is their bedroom. Take their hand and walk the room, touching each piece of furniture that brings function to the room. When you touch it, say what it is. After repetition through the days, hopefully your child will begin saying these things with you.

Touch - lamp; touch - bed; touch - dresser; touch - window; touch - closet; touch - nightstand; touch - light switch.

You can move on and do another room or you can stop. Repeat this exercise at least every day. Tell your child what room you'll add next into The Grounding Game. When you're ready and your child understands the game, add the bathroom. Touch the tub, towel holder, toilet, toilet paper holder, sink, shower, etc.

You are building a mental map into your child's mind which forms the function of each room. You can add touching the fluffy run at the base of the toilet if you'd like your child's mental map to include this piece. Softer, warmer things can help take the edge off the cold, porcelain bathroom. You can even prep the bathroom to be inviting before starting this game. Include a magazine holder with books, a child-friendly picture to look at, and colorful textiles. Touch all these things to help paint a full understanding of the bathroom.

Make sure you stay in the same order as you touch these things daily. The bathroom order should include the toilet activities in order of their eventual use. Toilet - books - toilet paper - sink - hand towel. If you include the toilet rug or step stool, start with those first. It will help your child ground their feet in the proper place before sitting down. Rug - toilet - picture (on the way across from toilet so your child turns the proper way to sit down) - books - toilet paper - sink - towel.

Think through how you want your home to be perceived and what you want your child to begin to function within your home. You definitely want a squishy potty seat, as well. Something soft and tactile, not hard and cold. Check out the Product Section for recommendations. This game can be transferred to the kitchen if you want your child to be able to get his own water from the fridge. You aren't telling him to do it. You are prepping the mental map in his mind to walk through the process over and over, before ever teaching him to get his own water. Cupboard - cups - fridge - water tap.

When you are ready to potty train, The Grounding Game would have familiarized your child with every household aspect of training, leaving them freer to focus on urge sensation and wardrobe functions. When the game is a familiar part of life, start doing the bathroom (more specifically the elimination portion of the bathroom) with your child a few times a day. Morning, lunch, dinner, and before bed. This will help build into their minds the idea of going to the bathroom every morning, after lunch, after dinner, and before bed.

Hang your PECS cards near the area of their use. When you are in the bathroom doing your Grounding Game, you can start to point to the PECS cards and add them into your words. Hopefully, there are some good ideas here to help prep your child and ease the transition of potty training. Again, offer what you think could work to your occupational therapist or pediatrician to get a full picture of the plan. Feel free to visit me on Facebook under the Laura Woj profile if you have more thoughts or questions!

Incentives

When considering incentives, think outside of the box. Children with special needs can see the world through a different lens. You may find that they don't care for things a typical child might, but care greatly for things that don't often matter to others. Before beginning potty training, make sure you find the right incentive. You cannot flip flop your incentive. It needs to be something your child will work for and you must be 100 percent sure, before you start.

Perhaps your child LOVES petting the dog. Maybe your child is absolutely gaga over yogurt! Maybe the best thing in the world that your child could do is swing in the backyard or play in the sandbox. These are innocent things, but children can find the most amazing pleasures in the simple things in life. Think outside of the box.

If you child's favorite food has been yogurt, then guess what? Yogurt could be what they work for. Yogurt is not a controlled substance and is earned by sitting on the toilet. Remember our Potty Tracker? If you child is sitting on the toilet during their interval, they DO have stuff in them that needs to come out. And if they sit until you say they are done, they get that yogurt.

Dr. Pat Mirenda, PhD has much to say that can help parents potty training those with special needs. Check out https://actcommunity.ca for more information.

Why In the World…

Why in the world does my potty training toddler poop or pee as soon as we get a trainer or clothing on, even after we've sat on the toilet for ever??

Some parents tell me their children are potty training just fine, but when they put a trainer on them, the kid just pees or poops in them and doesn't seem to care. Well, why should he? This was how it always was before. He never had to care about pooping in this diaper. Only you cared. He is just slipping back into old habits.

You imagine that since you have introduced this concept of using the bathroom, your child has locked onto it and can quickly see the benefits of staying clean. Guess what? He never cared before! He doesn't know about germs and he hasn't had thirty years of the opposite physical conditioning. In fact, his body and mental conditioning has always been to "let go" when being hugged by clothing, so get ready to watch like a hawk when that little one gets dressed! The act of dressing, itself, could be triggering a biological (Pavlovian) response in him! However, you will certainly be much better off using trainers instead of underwear if you have a child struggling with this conditioning. Whether it is training pants or underwear, your kid may not care either way if he wets or poops. Trainers contain things better. Much better. Thin,

186

mildly absorbent, waterproof trainers will contain stuff even better and make your life easier.

Waterproof trainers also hold wetness on the child's side, upping the wet feeling they will get when they pee. One thing is for certain though. You need to stay the course and re-train in undies. "Naked" is not a sustainable way of living!

Why in the world does my kid pee her pants right after I just asked her if she needed to pee? She told me "no," then peed her pants within a minute!

It's because you just brought up the subject. She wasn't thinking about it earlier. Then you asked! Maybe she didn't really need to pee, but after you asked the question, it brought about a mental connection and awareness to her body and she realized she actually could pee! And so you have an accident. If you've done the Potty Tracker and know her interval, simply tell her to sit at that time.

Why in the world does my child pee as soon as we get in the car, even though I made him try to pee before we left?

You might be checking all the boxes and asking before you leave the house, but you can still end up in this situation. You tell them to try, they sit there, nothing much happens, and you leave. Now you get in the car and start to drive away and two minutes down the road they are screaming they need to go pee! Yes, we are doing this to ourselves. You can do one of two things. You could keep asking. But instead, have your child try to go to the bathroom ten minutes before leaving the house, without them knowing you are leaving. Watch them like a hawk after you do ask, because they could tell you "no," then have an accident. At least it's an accident at home, rather than in the car. The other option is to not say a word. Just buckle that little tyke up and head off. Again, if you completed the Potty Tracker, you will know when your child will have to eliminate and you can plan accordingly. Take the streets when possible and have a car plan (travel toilet) ready, but don't even mention it. Talking about it and asking if they have to go gets them thinking about it, which gets them needing to go! But remember, every accident is one step closer to being potty trained. It is nothing more than a valuable learning experience!

Why in the world does my child hide to poop?

Kids are smart. Your child has already picked up on the fact that this is a private thing. But in addition, most hiding kids are also squatting to poop! That's a tough position to copy with all our toilet and mini potty options! They may also feel a little vulnerable when pooping, causing them to hide. You can let your child hide his potty and get one that is super low. I like the Prince Lionheart pottyPOD. Its shape naturally separates the legs and helps with a squat. You can get a deeper squat by putting a book under each foot, but this is tough to do for a kid who needs privacy. You should tell your kid he is welcome to put the potty ANYWHERE he feels most comfortable and if that is in a closet, then so be it. You could also tell him how squatting helps the poop come out. Teach him to squat over the potty. Act like you don't know he already does this and you'll boost his self-esteem! You could also make a private, personal potty area in your home for him. Hang or clamp sheets up to create a private space for them. Your toddler will love the attention and consideration you're giving him and may be intrigued enough to use his new personal space!

Why in the world will my child simply refuse to sit on the potty! She is three and I've tried every bribe possible!

Sit your child down at the table. Offer her a drink and have one yourself. Settle in for a nice, but serious conversation. Ask her what the deal is. Don't offer up much info at this point. Let her answer you. It might take a bit. Level with her. Be kind, but truthful. Tell her you think she is completely capable of doing this and that we can't be in diapers forever. You can't keep buying them. What will she do when they are gone? LET HER come up with a solution. That's the truth. One day, there will be no more diapers and she's going to have to figure this out. You can't do anything else for her. You can support her, but this is her dilemma. See how the conversation unfolds. Maybe you back off and have another conversation later or maybe you set a date when you won't be able to buy diapers anymore. Don't be afraid. Just open up a conversation. Make sure she understands that she is going to have a problem to solve when diapers are not provided anymore. Many times, this will get a child to begin to cooperate. Making them responsible for themselves helps them feel more independent, which is why they are not sitting on the toilet in the first place.

Product Section

If you're wondering what to buy, check out these products first. Make the decision that fits best within your family and your budget. All of these products are sturdy enough to be used through multiple children, which is a benefit built into the price. Some of these products can go beyond potty training, as well! BONUS!

I've put much research into the different goods out there and although there are more options, these are my final choices. The products themselves are top-notch, but the ones that made my list also come from family-owned-and-operated companies with great business ethics.

The pottyPOD®

The pottyPOD®
By Prince Lionheart®

I know I talk often about the mini potty you should have in your home. There are many, many brands and styles to choose from, so here's what you want to look for in a tiny toilet.

Wide base

You want the potty to be sturdy and comfortable for your toddler. They should feel secure and it shouldn't wobble on the floor. A low-to-the-ground toilet with a wide base gives kids the feeling and position they need to help copy a squat. If they are sitting for a long time, you want something comfortable, as well.

After looking at many options, I'd like to point out the pottyPOD® from Prince Lionheart®. It has a quick dump cup and splash guard like other toilets, but there are a few things that just set it apart. I'm NOT referring to the pottyPOD Basix®, which sells for about $25. The "Basix" is missing some of these features I mention below, but this is a great travel potty for tailgaters or car trips. It is quite a bit smaller and more compact. The main pottyPOD™ goes for about $50 and is way more stocked on features than other toilets. Here are my top reasons why I recommend this over other potties:

•   Adjustable height - The base of this toilet can change depending on your needs. If you plan on having a second child, this is a great benefit! Set the toilet where your children are comfortable!

- Splash guard or not! - The splash guard is removable, but it can also be easily flipped back for girls, lessening the chance you will lose it. This means it's great for multiple genders and multiple children. Just store it and await your next arrival!
- Wide and sturdy base - This toilet is solid! It's well-made with great materials. It feels much better quality than the toilets made by toy companies and it doesn't rock or shift when your toddler sits on it. The plastic is thicker and more solid. Corners weren't cut on design or materials when they designed the pottyPOD®.
- SQUISH! - This toilet has an AMAZING, specialized squishy material that the seat is made of. It's soft, comfy, and won't feel cold when your kid sits down! But don't be fooled when I say "squish." It's solid AND soft. Your little one will feel secure when this potty seat gives their bum a hug.
- It's anti-microbial - I know, right? ANTI-MICROBIAL! This is quite possibly the only potty on the market that has an EPA-approved additive to the dump cup, which inhibits the growth of microorganisms. This toilet is definitely a parent's best friend!

This toilet is the Cadillac of all mini potty goodness. It won't be your travel potty; it will be your go-to potty. Your in-it-for-the-long-haul, multi-child, let friends borrow it kind of potty.

Travel potties in the Prince Lionheart® range

The pottyPOD Basix® has the same look as the pottyPOD®, but with an all plastic top and bottom - no squish. Also great for travel is the pottyPOD Squish®, a toilet seat reducer that has the same great squishy foam as the big pottyPOD®. It's light weight and can be used on the big toilet at home or when heading out.

The UPPY2™ and FaucetEXTENDER™

UPPY2™ and FaucetEXTENDER™

These two products are a team. They just fit together so well! They are the Hygiene Team! Make it easy for kids to wash their hands and they will.

The UPPY2™ is the better step stool. It just goes higher than the rest. Most two-step stools take the height of a regular stool and cut it in half, giving you two steps, with just a touch more height. The UPPY2™ will get your toddler up there!

Couple the UPPY2™ with a FaucetEXTENDER™ and you have a winning team! There are faucet extenders out there, but this one wins. It can attach to standard or gooseneck faucets. It sports two different attachment points, one in the back and one on top. Other faucet extenders only attach in the back, making them suitable for a standard bathroom faucet. Try them in the kitchen and they fail you.

I recommend starting your potty training journey in a limited space. Some educators tell you to lock yourself in the bathroom, but I think it is more practical to use the main hub of your house, so you can still function. This usually means a combo of living room and kitchen, or living room, dining room, and kitchen. With the FaucetEXTENDER™, you will be able to wash hands on the premises, close to your mini toilet and potty training command center.

Prince Lionheart's® UPPY2™ and FaucetEXTENDER™ will get you washing like a champ in the kitchen or bath. When you start with great hygiene practices at a young age, you are giving them a skill they will carry with them forever.

The Squattypottymus™

SquattyPottymus™

Squatty Potty definitely listens to their customers! They began getting frequent calls requesting a taller stool that could help children transition from diapers to the toilet. As we discussed earlier, pooping can be a huge issue for kids. They can be afraid of falling in the toilet or uncomfortable with the position necessary to use it. Feet dangling in the air is a far cry from what they are used to. In some cases, this anxiety can lead to children holding poop in, which can back them up and lead to constipation.

That is what inspired the concept of the SquattyPottymus™, a taller stool which small children could climb on and use the toilet. It is accompanied by an ergonomic seat which makes it comfortable and secure for them. The SquattyPottymus™ stool encourages a natural squat, opening their little colon for an easier and more effective poop. The seat helps to take away the fear of the big hole in the toilet as it cradles them into a very comfortable experience and they feel safe.

The SquattyPottymus™ comes with a cap to extend the height of the stool to accommodate different toilet heights or smaller children. As a child grows, the stool adjusts by removing the cap. It is designed for ages two to eight years.

Squatty Potty has been contacted by several pediatricians requesting Squatty Potty to design something to aid in toilet training. They see many issues with children because of fear and simply not being in the right posture/position that they should be. I am very optimistic that the SquattyPottymus™ can help start kids out safe and secure and help to prevent many of the issues that children face with poor elimination. The potty stool comes with the toilet seat reducer and retails for around $60.

Hero Undies

By Super Undies®

Extra Waterproof Shield

**Gussets inside offer
more waterproof protection**

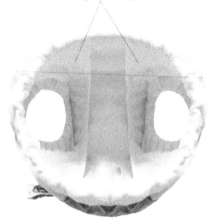

**Insert Sets Come in
a Bamboo Blend or Microfiber**

**A Hero Undies Insert Set comes
with two inserts that join together**

Hero Undies
By Super Undies®

As fas as reusable bedwetting pants go, you don't get any better than these. There are only a few cloth bedwetting products on the market to choose from. Disposable products are available at every big-box store, but they get more expensive the bigger you get and they give you fewer in each pack as you size up. With potty training, you can gauge how long you may be in that playing field, but with bedwetting there is no way to tell. Some people find themselves dealing with bedwetting for a year, while others deal with it for seven years. All of a sudden, reusable cloth is looking like a better idea.

Hero Undies are about $25 for the shell. Then, you buy the insert. Your Hero Undies are where the triple waterproofing comes from and your Insert Set is where the absorbency comes from. These two items make a force to reckon with! Many children I know hate the idea of wearing a disposable product. They feel it carries the stigma of being a baby, because they view it as a "baby diaper." Going to cloth can help children hold on to their dignity in a sense. It can also help eliminate bedwetting.

A cloth overnight option can help a child wake up when bedwetting, by heightening the feeling of "something happening" down there. Sometimes, disposables do too good a job in making a child feel dry. A child will only feel wet

in cloth if he is waking up when he wets. Otherwise, the wet feeling will be lost through sleep. This is ideal, letting kids sleep when they really need it, but waking them up if there is even a chance they could combat bedwetting naturally. Explore Hero Undies more thoroughly at SuperUndies.com to see videos of how they work.

Pull-on Undies 2.0
By Super Undies®

These potty training pants are trim and beautifully constructed, but first, they are made in America. That being said, if you were to hold one of these trainers in your hand with something you bought at a big-box store, there is simply no comparison. Here are the top reasons these trainers are better than the average:

- Stretchy side tabs - Other trainers with side tabs use one layer of fabric and it is typically cotton. Pull-on Undies have two layers of fabric per tab and it is a stretchy smooth Lycra fabric. Those side tabs hug a toddler's hip for a great fit and they stay in place.
- Elastic recovery - You will notice in standard training pants that their choice of fabric is cotton (or cheaper polyester that feels like cotton), which has some stretch, but no recovery. That means when the product is stretched out, it doesn't come back in until you wash and dry it. This causes the underwear to sag while they are on your toddler. Super Undies Lycra blend fabrics have stretch and recovery at the same time!
- Waterproof through the wet zone - The main body of these Undies is waterproof and that means less mess for expensive items. You can save your car seat, carpet, and couch from needing to be replaced after potty training days are over.

- Slight absorbency - Pull-on Undies have two layers of microfiber absorbency inside. This is enough to absorb 160 milliliters of fluid or almost a whole "pee." Notice I said almost. The absorbency is not designed as a diaper and won't absorb it ALL. But since the body of the trainer is waterproof, it keeps the wetness on the child's side. Imagine that. Not being fully absorbent, but still being waterproof. That combination is going to give your child a pretty squishy butt and that's exactly what we want when potty training!
- Lets your toddler feel the wetness - The inner fabric is not a stay-dry fabric. Your tyke is going to KNOW if they just peed!
- Inner pocket for more absorbency – Sometimes, you just need a break. Sometimes, you know you'll be in the car for a long time. Sometimes, you need to get on a plane. Sometimes, you might be going to visit your snooty friend who has a perfect house. But remember? Going back into a diaper is not an option. Putting an insert into the Pull-on Undies is an option! These Pull-on Undies Boosters are made of two layers of microfiber and can absorb an additional 160 milliliters. That's doubling the absorbency of the trainer, making them into mini diapers! But only when YOU say so.

These Pull-on Undies are "Daycare Approved" and run about $19 apiece. You can get them on sale and find package deals on the internet. If you invest in better quality trainers, plan on selling them used on eBay or a buy-sell-trade Facebook page of that brand. Trainers that are made in America hold a resale value that is surprising. You could easily get half your money back when you're done!

"When you think to yourself, 'I WISH I wasn't potty training right now!' it's time to use an insert."

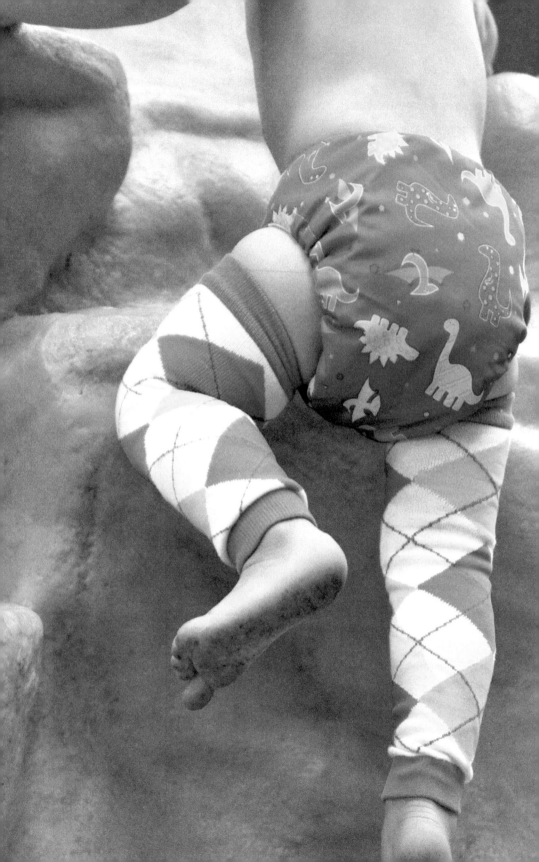

Baby Leggings
By Imagine Baby Products®

Potty training young? Potty training in the cold? Imagine's Baby Leggings can keep your little one's legs toasty warm. They are perfect for chilly days, windy strollers, or air-conditioned spaces.

These leggings are more than just cute though. They also help keep baby clean and scrape-free. When you're in the naked days of potty training, these leggings will not only keep your child from getting too drafty, but they can help reduce the shock of an accident on bare skin, by acting more like pants.

You will find that you can use these Baby Leggings long after potty training. If you find yourself in days that have chilly mornings but warm afternoons, Baby Leggings double as arm warmers to replace a bulky jacket.

USA MADE ★ Herb In

BALM! Baby

SPRAY that
BOTTOM!

[Diaper Spray / 1st Aid]

4 fl. oz. (e 120 mL)

Body Container ★ Vegan ★ ER

Spray That Bottom!
By Balm! Baby®

This spray ointment is made of a strong infusion of the earth's most healing herbs and Hawaii's most healing oils. It is a spray form of Balm! Baby's® best selling 1st Aid Balm. It is 100% natural and organic. Not only is it great for your little one's bum, but it can pull doubly duty and be used to sooth eczema, diaper rash, bug bites, itchy or dry skin, cradle cap, postpartum owies, hemorrhoids, scrapes, bruises, stinky arm pits, and even just to wash hands.

Now that I've overwhelmed you with it's magical properties, here's how to use it.

For wiping – Spray (or have little one spray) a few spritzes onto the toilet paper that will be used. Wipe butt.

For irritation that already exists – clean the affected area by spraying skin or toilet paper with Spray That Bottom!.

That's it! Teach your child to wipe until the toilet paper comes back clean. The spray will clean their bottom end, and condition their skin. It will help prevent irritation and redness, even if wiping conditions are not ideal. It's like a baby's backside first aid kit all in one bottle!

You can find Spray That Bottom! on SuperUndies.com. As a side note, Elevated, makers of the Balm Baby product line, make amazing skin care and wellness products too. I believe in this company so much that my personal facial cleaners, toner, toothpaste, and deodorant come from them. Their commitment to ethical business practices and sustainable packaging is unparallel to any other brand I am aware of.

We'd like to thank Blooming Lily Photography for the beautiful pictures she provided us with.

Ready to potty train? Me too! See you on Facebook at Scaredy Cat Potty Training

CPSIA information can be obtained
at www.ICGtesting.com
Printed in the USA
BVOW11s2246010917
493820BV00008B/8/P